The American Warrior

The
AMERICAN
WARRIOR

EDITED BY

Chris Morris and Janet Morris

Duane Elms, Research Director
Richard Groller, Chief Researcher

Cover design by Linda Kosarin

Interior design by Richard Oriolo

Library of Congress Cataloging-in-Publication Data

The American warrior / edited by Chris Morris and Janet Morris.
  —1st ed.
    p. cm.
  ISBN: 0-681-41401-4
    1. Sociology, Military—United States. 2. United States—History, Military—20th century. 3. Soldiers—United States—Biography. 4. United States—Armed Forces—Biography.
  I. Morris, Chris, 1946–   . II. Morris, Janet, 1946–
  U21.5. A48   1992
  306.2′7′0973—dc20   92-19825
                                                              CIP

Printed in the United States of America

First Edition

0 9 8 7 6 5 4 3 2 1

This book is for the guardians of freedom. Then. Now. And those in years to come.

This book is for the caretakers of ideas and ideals who move us to sacrifice, whether with words or deeds. Gilgamesh was a creation of the ancient mind; Sargon of Akkad marched to the sea with that image of greatness to guide him. Homer wrote a morality play for politicians, a manual for leaders, a treatise on soldiering; Alexander the Great carried it with him as he conquered the known world.

Many who should have had their say in these pages couldn't contribute. Some are dead. Some are too busy doing what they do. Some are constrained by security considerations. Some wouldn't think of it. Some couldn't find the words. Some of the best we know don't believe they are qualified. And others don't believe there is—or should be—a warrior class, especially not in a democratic society, and that the very idea is dangerous.

To these last, most of all, we offer this text. At the end of such a bloody century, we must take a moment to honor our dead and ask our living "What did it mean?" "Was it worth it?" "Why did you do it?" "Who are you?"

And, lastly, "Who are we?"

If we truly are becoming something different, something new, something better upon the earth, it will be these caretakers among us who are the first to know.

Acknowledgments

The editors wish to express their gratitude to those who contributed to and/or participated in the conception and execution of this project, and to the compilation of this text.

During the time that this work was in progress, the Berlin Wall came down, Eastern Europe broke away from the Soviet Union and repudiated the Warsaw Pact, Saddam Hussein invaded Kuwait, the United States and its allies went to war in the Persian Gulf, the Soviet Union renounced Communism, the Baltic Republics became free and sovereign states, the Russian Republic under Yeltsin began its transformation, the Soviet Union underwent an attempted coup, the Ukraine, Byelorussia, and other states declared independence, the PLO and Israel began peace talks, the Russian Republic and its allies announced the dissolution of the Soviet Union and the formation of the Commonwealth of Independent States, Mikhail Gorbachev retired from power, and the groundwork was laid by the superpowers for the dismantlement of nuclear weapons.

Consequently, many of the people who had announced their intention to contribute to this book became extremely busy and remained so during the entire time, from Christmas 1989 until New Year's Day of 1992, that the project was in preparation.

That so many of our original contributors did find time to respond is in itself an example of the spirit we hoped to capture.

We thank those people who, against all odds, managed to collect their thoughts and express their views in this time of furiously paced change.

Our thanks also go to Jim Morris (no relation) who worked on this project during conceptual stages, but finally contented himself with becoming a contributor. Jim's suggestions produced some fine results, and he gave time freely. His piece is one of the more eloquent statements made by those of his generation. Our thoughts go with you, friend, wherever you roam. Long may you wave.

This manuscript could not have been completed without the constant, steady support of Duane Elms, who stood in as editor when we were stuck in the Pentagon, over our heads with other duties, traveling overseas, or simply swamped with work. Duane created the mailing list from our notes, did the horse work of solicitation, received and entered documents, and dealt with the day-to-day problems of acquiring and organizing material at a time when the U.S. military-industrial complex was undergoing an unprecedented convulsion. Duane, we literally could not have done this without you.

The text would not have its breadth or depth without the continual help, throughout its compilation, of Major Richard Groller (USAR), who suggested contributors and offered unflagging assistance. Rich suggested authors, kept in touch with all of his people for status reports on work in progress, suggested additional contributors when some original participants had to withdraw, and generally ran herd on all of his contacts. Rich Groller's success rate on acquiring finished contributions from his candidates was the greatest of anyone helping develop contributions. He also had access to an echelon of personnel that none of the rest of us could reach. Once again, Rich, you proved to be an invaluable asset.

Lastly, and perhaps most importantly, we must thank Pam Altschul. For this project, Pam, only your continued enthusiasm—even when ours had flagged—guaranteed success.

Contents

Introduction

As with all truly difficult enterprises, this one began innocently enough, during one Christmas holiday when we had a former Special Forces major turned writer-journalist and his wife as our houseguests. The Berlin Wall had just fallen.

It seemed simple, at the time: an era of superpower conflict called the Cold War and its bilateral balance was clearly ending. The question was, what did this change mean to the United States, to the international community, and to the Third World?

There was clearly no answer. Truth would be arrived at by event and happenstance. However, there seemed to us to be a need for informal debate, a review of the ground covered in forty plus years of shadow conflict.

We'd poll our friends, asking those who were survivors of declared and undeclared wars, conflicts, little wars (civil wars, bush wars, border disputes, covert actions), and peacekeeping missions and see who among us believed that the downing of the Berlin Wall was signaling an end to all conflict, a great peace dividend, and amity among humankind forever after, as the press and the politicians were telling us to believe.

Most of our acquaintances, the four of us were sure, were reacting with as much skepticism as we. None of us that Christmas in 1989 doubted that the Middle East would flare into open violence as the superpowers relaxed their grip. We just weren't sure when, or how, or who first. We saw signs of destabilization in the very cessation of the small wars among superpower client states, as funding was abruptly cut off by the Soviet Union and the United States. We expected the area of Third World disputes, euphemistically called LIC (Low-Intensity Conflict), finally to get the attention we felt it deserved.

First to come into focus would be the Middle East, then perhaps the nuclearization of India/Pakistan or the Pacific Rim, and of course one couldn't forget Southeast Asia or the South American and African nations.

We were right about the Middle East, even about Iraq as a protagonist, but then, that was obvious it seems in retrospect. However, our concern went deeper than whether Saddam would go over the border or North Korea would go nuclear, or whether the attempts of Malaysia, Singapore, and their neighbors to buy used F-5 fighter planes on the gray market meant that the Pacific Rim nations were getting ready for a confrontation when mainland China took over Hong Kong.

Our doubts about the world achieving and maintaining geopolitical stability in our lifetimes went deeper. None of us truly believed that humankind could or would survive without a defined threat against which to marshal forces, define self, or stand united. History was on the side of violence, partisanship, and momentum. So, too, was economics: too much of the gross national product of the developed countries was dependent on the conflict-oriented consumption of Third World countries.

2

But we could agree on little else. So we spent Christmas Day making a list of those whose opinions we respected. In that instant, we thought many of our high-echelon contacts would wish to voice their opinions in the vacuum we perceived to be present in popular thoughts on the future of us all.

That initial list of contributors has changed greatly since then. So has the perception of humanity's future. For those of us who watch or become embroiled in international conflict and world events, a few things have become clear as of this first day of 1992:

1. The world's governing bureaucracies, formed in response to decades of sameness, defined threats, and stable enemies, continue to be inadequate to, if not paralyzed by the rate of change in the destabilized international environment.
2. The reactive, rather than proactive, nature of large governments has created a continuing state of unpreparedness, an unwillingness to adapt to change, and thus an impotency belied by the single clear-cut triumph of consensus in the case of Iraq's invasion of Kuwait.
3. The present rate of change itself supports inaction as a strategy of large governmental systems: highly placed bureaucrats assume that if they can ignore—or fail to react to—changes they don't like for a sufficient time, another, more acceptable reality will emerge.

Like peace in the Middle East, the results are up to people. A few people, not a lot of people. Sometimes we forget how few the decision makers really are, and how much their personal beliefs and capabilities affect history as it flows over us all.

The contributors who spoke to our list of questions are drawn from those few who made a difference—most because they were on the sharp end of conflicts, some because they fought behind the lines to give those at the front the critical advantages that mean the difference between winning and losing: clear policy, superior strategy, workable doctrine, technological superiority, timely intelligence, operationally viable tactics, field support.

Looking out the window at the Pentagon, one wonders whether all the combined skills of the past will be equal to the challenges of our future. Do we suddenly need different skills, a different ethic, a different sensibility? Is our world changing too fast for humankind to adapt? Can we grasp the opportunities at hand, or will they slip away? Will we end up once again nose to nose with a mortal enemy because we are simply incapable of living without an enemy, without a threat? And will we create such an enemy where none exists because we must have one to motivate a society accustomed to being driven by threat?

The editors recently returned from Moscow, where we guided a group of technology evaluators on an assessment of Russian capability to turn the high-technology of their military-industrial complex to peaceful uses. When we got off the plane at the Moscow airport, one of our party remarked, "So this is the Evil Empire?" He was disappointed by the lack of threat in evidence there. He continued to be disappointed by a lack of menace and hostility throughout the trip.

Soon after arriving back home, we received a phone call from one of our group, a man who is considered by many in the defense establishment to be a "national treasure." In order to take him to Moscow we had had to obtain special interagency courtesies, promise never to leave him alone with a Russian, and see to it that Russians were unable to maintain or continue contact with him thereafter.

4

The man was calling to discuss the lack of response by our government to the group's report.

In frustration, our friend asked, "Have we lost sight of our mission?"

Right now, we don't know the answer to that question. The truth may be intricately involved with the need to define a threat, have an enemy, limit change, and the difficulty of adaptation to change. Maybe by the time you read this, the answer will be clearer, as far as the United States and its place in history are concerned. Whatever that answer is, geopolitically, the people who contributed to this volume know the answer, for themselves. For each one it is a matter of pride and soul, honor and duty, responsibility and accomplishment, sometimes in conflict, sometimes in accord.

We had hoped, and still do hope, that by compiling this group of personal statements, we would create a composite insight into the nature of the people who create the systems that seem to take on, but never actually acquire, an independent and somehow impersonal identity.

At the end of this epoch, and halfway across the threshold into a seemingly unmanageable complexity of possible futures, we need to know as much as we can about how we got here and in whom we have entrusted our fate for the difficult crossing ahead.

For we are making a crossing, and it is one in which our technological expertise, on which we have come to rely, cannot greatly help us. Our technology has drowned us in data. We are swamped with information. Our systems cannot assess what we know. We must decide, act, and move forward in a storm of uncertainty. Knowing only that we must choose, must be proactive, must shape the changes ahead, we are thrown back on the basic questions that have always decided our survival: Do we have constancy, clear purpose, perseverance?

Some of our contributors are grappling with these questions. Some are lost in the storm. Some are full of energy and some full of wisdom; very few have both. Many have been so deeply marked by their experiences that they are truly products of their eras. Some have hope; others have questions. Sometimes, their questions are more important than their answers. Sometimes, their answers reveal much more than was intended.

This book project was originally called "The Warrior Class." The title was carefully chosen to evoke emotion and cause debate. Although the title is now different, the debate remains. A number of the contributors have addressed the question of whether there is, or is not, a warrior class. We have chosen to preserve some of these modern answers to an age-old question.

We also have included a section called "The Overachievers." These men, despite clear directions from us to choose one or two questions from a list and answer them at a specified length, insisted on answering every question. Since this occurred more than once—and once it occurred after a long phone conversation in which we argued the matter with the contributor—we have decided to print all the questions along with each person's answers. In at least one case, the respondent felt that the body of questions represented a challenge he couldn't refuse. Another respondent felt that the body of questions had caused him to think about things he had never, in a long life of service, considered.

Sometimes questions can do that. Sometimes, they can haunt you or focus you. We tried to ask all the right questions, when we compiled *The American Warrior* solicitation.

But the single question that may well be the key to the nature of these sometimes extraordinary people was not asked by us. Rather, it was asked *of* us, during an early morning call from a sixty-seven-year-old retired Army colonel, William P. Schneider. Bill, a contributor to the book and a former military attaché at the U.S. Embassy, Moscow, was working with us on a joint report on our Moscow trip. The project was gargantuan. Everyone was exhausted, putting in eighteen-hour days without a break in sight.

Bill's cheerful voice on the phone said, "Good morning, and what are you going to do for your country today?"

A NOTE ON THE CREATION OF THE TEXT

The material in this text was compiled from a questionnaire sent to members of the foreign policy, military, and intelligence communities who were carefully chosen for their diversity of experience, rank, and points of view. The questions we asked them were meant to be difficult, evoke emotional responses, or cause a personal inventory of experience to take place. Each contributor represented here is a member of a self-selected group, each of whom had the courage to tackle this purposely difficult task, and the generosity of spirit to do so without regard to material compensation. They are a special subset—less than one-quarter of those who received the original questionnaire.

The contributors' responses themselves dictated the format in which the material is presented. The questions they chose to answer became the text's outline, and the way they answered those questions created debate and concensus within the larger volume, as well as causing the creation of the special section called *The Overachievers*.

Reading the American Warrior

The material is grouped by concept, and divided into six sections: Warriorship; Personal Commitment; Combat; The World; The

Future; and the Overachievers. Everywhere but in *the Overachievers*, the questions addressed by the authors in each section appear at the front of the section, followed by a brief introduction to the section; Each contributors' name precedes the contribution by that author; in the *Table of Contents*, under each section, contributors to that section are listed; some contributors appear in more than one section. In the last section, *The Overachievers*, contributors who appear nowhere else in the volume address sixteen questions in round table fashion; these questions are ordered as they were in the original questionnaire. A short *Biographies* section, profiling all contributors is included directly following the introduction, to allow readers the option of reading the text by author or authority, rather than subject, if they so choose. Although we have provided for the reader who may wish to read only the views of a particular author or subset of authors, or read only views on particular subjects or answers to specific questions, we recommend Lewis Carroll's venerable formula: "Start at the beginning, go to the end, and then stop."

Biographies

Most of the contributers to this volume could write books about their life experiences. These capsule biographies are meant only to introduce to the men and women who speak so eloquently for themselves in the following pages.

Colonel John Alexander, USA (Ret.): Colonel Alexander led Special Forces A-Teams in Vietnam, including SF A-Team 421, in which each American was protected by mercenary Cambodians and Vietnamese irregulars. He was a member of Delta Task Force and the Intelligence and Security Command. He is currently manager of anti-materiel technology at Los Alamos National Laboratory. John is a co-author of *Warrior's Edge* and *Nonlethal Force*.

Lt. Col. Mark Barent, USAF (Ret.): Mark Barent served in the Air Force for more than twenty years, first as an enlisted man and then as an officer. He has logged 4,350 hours of flying time, over 1,000 of them in combat. During his three Vietnam tours, Barent earned not only the Silver star, but two Distinguished Flying Crosses, over two dozen air medals, the Bronze Star, the Vietnamese Cross of Gallantry, and the Legion of

Merit. He is the author of *Rolling Thunder* and the forthcoming *Steel Tiger*.

Major William H. Burgess III, USA: Major Burgess is a Special Forces officer with the 3rd Special Forces Group (Airborne) at Fort Bragg, North Carolina. He served as a 3rd Group company commander in the Middle East during Operation Desert Storm. Major Burgess is a graduate of OCS, the Special Forces Officer Course, the Infantry and Military Intelligence officers advanced courses, Command and General Staff College, and has written extensively on the Special Forces.

Cpt. Mitchell Burnside Clapp, USAF: Captain Clapp graduated from MIT in 1984 with Bachelor's degrees in Russian, Aeronautics and Astronautics, and Physics, and a Master's degree in Aeronautics and Astronautics. He is also a graduate of the U.S. Air Force Test Pilot School and the Squadron Officers School. Currently, he is Chief of Curriculum Reports and Instructor, USAF Test Pilot School. He has flown over 30 types of military aircraft, principally the F-4 and A-7.

Dr. Ray Cline: Dr. Cline is a former Deputy Director for Intelligence of the Central Intelligence Agency and a Professor of International Relations at Georgetown University.

Spec-5 David Drake, USA (Ret.): David spent much longer in Vietnam than the eighteen months he served. He's a military historian and a fluent linguist who reads Roman writers in Latin. He has become very successful writing military science fiction.

1st Lt. Clifford R. Fagan, USA: Lt. Fagan is a Platoon Leader for a TOW anti-tank platoon. He served in Panama during the Noriega crisis and was Crisis Action/Operations Officer/USSOUTHCOM Joint Operations Center.

Cpt. Linda A. Gorsuch, USA: Captain Gorsuch is currently the editor of the *Military Intelligence Professional Bulletin.*

Major Richard Groller, (USAR): Major Groller is a former Army Intelligence officer, now attached to DIA. During his 11 years active duty, he was a principal advisor to U.S. Space Command on space force enhancement to military operations and space-based tactical intelligence. He is a co-author of *Warrior's Edge.*

Steve Hartov, IDF (Ret.): Steve Hartov is currently director of the Airborne Operations Group, an organization of Allied personnel that arranges joint training operations overseas. His first novel was published in hardcover in spring, 1992. He is a former Israeli paratrooper, and often serves as a technical and weapons advisor on action-adventure films.

Colonel Michael Hayden, USAF: Colonel Hayden was Director of Defense Policy at the National Security Council at the time this book was written. Mike has moved on to become Chief of the Air Force Secretary's Group.

Cpt. D.L. "Pappy" Hicks USA (Ret.): Captain Hicks served in combat in Korea, Laos, and Vietnam. He also collected covert intelligence in Africa, Germany, Iran. He is the author of numerous westerns and adventure books.

Stacey Jenkins: Stacey grew up in a military family and joined the Army at 17. She was trained as a medic and served for three years in Germany before leaving the service.

Major David P. Kutchinski, USA (Ret.): Major Kutchinski was a member of the Special Forces, Military Intelligence, and a U.S. Army Special Forces electronic warfare systems architect. He was instrumental in bringing electronic warfare techniques to Special Forces. He has been an FBI undercover agent and is a certified instructor in small arms use.

SFC Ronald E. McGuire, USA (Ret.): Sergeant McGuire spent 20 years as an electronics specialist in the Army Security Agency.

1st Lt. Michelle Miller: Lieutenant Miller was attached to the 128th Combat Support Hospital in Saudi Arabia during the Persian Gulf War. She is currently serving on active duty at the 2nd Field Hospital, Bremerhaven, Germany.

Major Tom Moore, USAR: Tom Moore was, at the time his contribution was written, a legislative assistant for military affairs to Wyoming Senator Malcolm Wallop (R). He is a major in the Army Reserves. He's also a writer, not only of some memorable Wallop speeches and other nonfiction, but of a novel we hope will soon see print. By the time this is published, we expect he will have joined the White House staff.

Major Jim Morris, USA (Ret.): Jim Morris is a retired Special Forces major. His books on Vietnam are some of the most highly acclaimed ever written about that war. He writes frequently for *Soldier of Fortune* and other publications.

Mr. Paul O'Keefe, USAR: Mr. O'Keefe was commissioned in the Military Intelligence Reserve and has served both as an officer and civilian for over 28 years.

Mr. Gary O'Neal, USA: Warrant Officer O'Neal along with Michael Echani developed the Hand-To-Hand Combat, Special Weapons School for instructors. As a Ranger, Mr. O'Neal served 68 months in combat, mostly with Special Operations units. He has served as an instructor in Special Operations units, Military Freefall (HALO), and SCUBA School. He was one of the founders of the U.S. Army S. E. R. E. School with long time friend Col. Nick Rowe. He has been on the world-famous U.S. Army Parachute team, the Golden Knights, and has over 6,000 freefall jumps to his credit.

Major Steve Pope: Major Pope is a serving Signals Officer in the Canadian armed forces. He has been Head Signals Officer Training at the Canadian Forces School of Communications and Electronics.

Lt. Col. Neil L. Putz, USA: Colonel Putz is a graduate of the United States Military Academy at West Point, the U.S. Army Airborne and Ranger courses, the Signal Corps Basic and Advanced Courses, and the U.S. Army Command and General Staff College. He has a Master's degree in Systems Technology (Command, Control, and Communications) from the Naval Postgraduate School, Monterey, California.

Major Michael C. Redmond, USAR: Major Redmond received her commission through the ROTC program at the Brooklyn Polytechnic Institute and is now at the 1154th USARF School at Fort Totten.

SFC Barry Rhodes, USA: Sergeant Rhodes is currently split between 519th Military Intelligence Battalion and 319th Military Intelligence Battalion as NCO for both. He is an Intelligence Analyst (98G), a SF Medic, a Russian Linguist, and a Survival Instructor. He shot at national-level marksmanship competitions on the All-Guard Team and was the first man to solo-hike the Continental Divide from Canada to Mexico.

Lt. Col. Charles L. Rosenfeld, Oregon Army National Guard: Lieutenant Rosenfeld is commander of the 82nd Rear Area Operations Center, Oregon Army National Guard. He was commissioned into Military Intelligence Branch in Caracas, Venezuela, in 1968. In civilian life, Dr. Charles Rosenfeld is a Geo-sciences professor at Oregon State University. Colonel Rosenfeld served as a Visiting Professor at the U.S. Military Academy in 1990.

Colonel William P. Schneider, USA (Ret.): Bill Schneider attended West Point, served as Army Attaché in the Soviet Union, specialized in Soviet nuclear forces, and still speaks fluent Russian.

Dr. Thomas Starke: Dr. Starke is director of the Strategic Initiatives program at Los Alamos National Laboratory. He is both a visionary and a manager whose job currently involves retargeting the agenda of one of the most powerful of the national laboratories.

Brig. Gen. John F. Stewart, Jr., USA: General Stewart is currently Assistant Deputy Chief of Staff for Intelligence and Commanding General, U.S. Army Intelligence Agency. He has experience and decorations far too numerous to list here.

Brig. Gen. James Teal, Jr., USA (Ret.): During his thirty-two years in the Army, General Teal served in Korea, Japan, Vietnam, Panama Canal Zone, Germany, and the United States. He is a graduate of the Army's Command and General School and the Army War College and served as the Deputy Chief of Staff for Intelligence at the U.S. Army Forces Command. He is now with Andrew Corporation as Director of Business Development for the Government Products Group.

Commander Charles Edward Thompson, USN (Ret.):
Commander Thompson has served in the Air Force, the Army, and the Navy where he completed Aviation Officer Candidate School and accumulated more than 2,000 flight hours and more than 600 carrier landings in the A6A bomber and EA6B electronic warfare aircraft. Commander Thompson saw combat in Grenada and participated in the air strikes on Syrian positions in Lebanon in December 1983. His decorations include the Defense Meritorious Service Medal, the Navy Distinguished Service Medal, six Air Medals, the Navy Commendation Medal with Combat V, three Navy Achievement Medals, six Navy-Marine Expeditionary Medals, and others.

Lt. Gen. Richard G. Trefry, USA (Ret.): General Trefry was appointed as the Military Assistant to the President and Director, White House Military Office, on January 11, 1990. He also served as Inspector General of the U.S. Army. His military decorations include: the Distinguished Service Medal (with Oak Leaf Cluster); Legion of Merit with USN V Device (with Gold Star); Meritorious Service Medal; and the Army Commendation Medal (with two Oak Leaf Clusters).

Cpt. Bill Vlcek, USAF: Captain Vlcek received his commission in June 1982. For the past four years he has been an Air Force ROTC instructor in Worcester, Massachusetts. The previous four and a half years were spent in a variety of positions related to the acquisition and management of command and control computer systems.

Brig. Gen. George J. Walker, USA (Ret.): General Walker served thirty-five and a half years in the Army before retiring in 1989. Twenty-seven years of his career was served in tactical and strategic intelligence assignments at every level of com-

15

mand. His most noteworthy assignments included: Chief of Staff and Deputy Commanding General, U.S. Army Intelligence and Security Command; Chief of Staff and Deputy Commandant, U.S. Army Intelligence Center and School, and Director of Intelligence, J2, Forces Command.

Mr. Bob Wall: Bob Wall is a retired officer of the Central Intelligence Agency. He will tell you that, while at the CIA, he invented the Phoenix covert action program that ran in Southeast Asia during the Vietnam era.

Lt. Cmdr. Michael J. Walsh, USN: Commander Walsh currently trains SEALs. Most information about such people is classified.

Colonel John Warden III, USAF: Colonel Warden is regarded by many as the most brilliant Air Force strategist currently serving in Washington. He is currently Special Assistant to the Vice President for National Security Affairs.

Lt. Gen. James A. Williams, USA (Ret.): General Williams graduated from the United States Military Academy in 1954 and retired from active duty in 1985 after more than thirty-one years of service, during which he became the first West Pointer to rise from lieutenant to lieutenant general in the field of intelligence. As a lieutenant colonel he served in Vietnam in 1969. During this tour General Williams was twice decorated for gallantry. In 1981, General Williams became Director, DIA, and Director, General Defense Intelligence Programs.

Sgt. Maj. J.D. "Rowdy" Yeats, USA (Ret.): As a Special Forces soldier in Vietnam with the Military Advisor Command Vietnam (MACV) Special Operations Group (SOG), Sergeant

Major Yeats participated in over 250 combat insertions and extractions (the majority under hostile fire), spending a total of thirty-six months in Vietnam. He retired from the army with over twenty-four years service, all in Special Forces.

Warriorship

1. Are warriors made, or are they born?

2. Describe the qualities a warrior must have to survive and prevail.

3. What are the emotional rewards of warriorship?

4. All successful warriors subscribe to an ethic of behavior, a code of honor. Some call this "common values" and others say it is a "sense of duty." Say what warriorship means to you. How do you see your role in society?

When we sent out the original solicitation for contributions to this book, it was entitled *The Warrior Class*. Many people who might otherwise not have contributed to this project may have done so because of the strong feelings that title evoked within members of the community. The debate over whether a warrior class exists or should exist rings through the following exploration of warriorship.

For every contributor who objected to the concepts attached to the words *warrior* and/or *class* (let alone the exponential increase in controversy derived from linking the two words), there was another who unabashedly answers to the name and has consciously associated himself with the group that takes the association seriously.

In choosing our contributors, we have been careful to weed out the armchair warriors, who faced their greatest danger in a bar against each other or out in the woods with loaded weapons on Fourth of July weekend.

We were hopeful that the people we chose would give us straight answers to hard questions. The result is this survey of warriorship, and its depth and breadth is a measure of the quality of this group. It is important to note that few of the contributors to this or any other section of this text viewed their experiences in a historical context, of the sort that academics might have chosen. Not that history is lacking here. It is omnipresent. But this is history seen from the center of the cyclone, not from far afield. This is history as history is understood by the people who make it, rather than history as seen by the biographers of figureheads who lay claim to shaping our destinies.

Cpt. D. L. "Pappy" Hicks:

I am an American fighting man, a warrior. I started the warrior trail in my twelfth summer when I got the name of Tladagi Isgongodeoski, crudely translated to mean "Panther Follower." That summer, World War II ended and some of the boys around home said they were disappointed the war ended before they could get into it. I said it, and I meant it.

I got my chance when I was seventeen years old and the Korean War started. I tried to join the army, the only service I wanted to be in. I wanted to be infantry. They said I was too young. I talked my father, a half-breed Tsalagi South Texas rancher and cowboy, into going with me to San Antonio and signing for me. My grandfather's old second cousin, Charlie Hicks, who was my Indian teacher, told me to get a war song and he would fix it so no one could steal it and use it against me. I though up a song:

Udalehi heleskaste, gilugeh!
Udalehi heleskaste, gilugeh!
Geste agenu yege!
Yelaste gega tadegea.

Enemy, beware, I come!
Enemy, beware, I come!
I have never failed.
My knife is thirsty.

Our people are Tsalagi, or what the whites and other Indians call the Cherokee.

I was a rifleman in Korea, 1951–52, and the first time I sang my war song, the white boys in the platoon went crazy. I am white-looking like my mother, and they called me a "white heathen" and to stop that barbaric stuff because God may come down and kill us all. I had to go off alone to sing my song. I never sang it in front of white people again.

After the war, I got my B. S. degree and Army commission from ROTC from Texas A & I University at Kingsville and went back on active duty as a second lieutenant of infantry. I am also a paratrooper. Because I had a CIB and combat ribbons from the Korean war as a second lieutenant, my peers started

21

calling me "Pappy." It stuck and even generals called me Pappy before it was over with.

My combat experience was also noted by a few other people who got me working in covert special projects. I trained a number of teams from other countries at Fort Bragg and went on operations with some of them in their own countries. Working out of Fort Bragg, I made my first trip to Southeast Asia on a project in 1960. That was in Laos. Over the years I worked with Special Forces, the Central Intelligence Agency, and even the State Department.

I worked best with the Rhade tribesman of the Central Highlands in South Vietnam. I spoke their language and knew a lot about their culture. I was in a highly classified project on one trip with my Montagnard warriors. We went after the Viet Cong leaders, their intelligence people, paymasters, political cadre, handbill makers, and anyone in leadership. We ambushed them on trails, went into safe houses in towns or their guarded camps, and anyplace else we could find them. We either captured them or left them in place, dead. I always figured that if a man did not want to get hurt, then he should stay at home with Mama and the baby. Our intelligence came from the Vietnamese and my Montagnard sources. It was also a rough, scary job fighting in the jungles and mountains alone with three to ten men, ambushing the enemy with little or no outside support. Air America, with some of the best pilots I have seen, were our primary support. When things got rough and it looked like we would not pull one off, our old chief scout would say, *"Hemi bi arang!"* "We shall prevail!" He was a real warrior to fight with.

We were good and it was finally decided to turn it into a U.S.-sponsored program for the South Vietnamese. The project finally became the Phung Hoang/Phoenix Program in December 1967.

After a time, I was finally adopted by Rhade in an official three-day ceremony. After the third day, the *mjao*, who we call a "medicine man," performed the ceremony to adopt me. *Mjao riue yang, mjao mdi ako. Ah, koa ako.* "The *mjao* called the spirits, and placed sacrifice blood on my head." I was made a member of their secret warrior society and they gave me the name Y Among, "Tiger." I still wear my brass bracelet, used when I was adopted, which is called a *kong*.

My Rhade brothers loved to hear my war song. They were warriors and understood. The free Chinese in Laos and the Hmong mountain tribesmen in Laos understood. Most important of all, I understood.

After my last trip to Southeast Asia, I spent over a year in Army hospitals, and I was given full retirement for physical disability, retiring me as a captain. I still miss being on active duty, even after all these years. I keep up with some of the military. I take my old walking cane and go where I can help. I have assisted the Miskito Indian contras in Central America, and I have worked with different Laos resistance and Vietnamese resistance groups. My country may have run out on our allies, but it is hard for me to run. A man lives and dies with honor, or he lives and dies very badly. I have a saying that a few people have heard—"I can die with honor, but I can't live with dishonor." I learned quickly in the Army that fellow officers do not like a man who really believes that. It scares hell out of many of them. And yes, if I could I would go with any group to help get American live POWs I know who are in Laos and Vietnam. I wouldn't be able to do much, maybe get in the way, but I would die happy.

One of the better things I have done since retirement was assist Major James "Big Jim" Morris, U. S. Army, Retired, and Don Scott get two hundred plus Vietnamese Montagnards out of refugee camps in Thailand and to the United States in 1976.

And when Desert Storm started and I was sitting at home in my easy chair watching Peter Arnett on TV making an ass out of himself working as the propagandist for Saddam Hussein, I felt like I was AWOL. I had been in two wars in this century and here I was sitting in Troup, Texas, and not part of this one.

Much of the general public look upon men who call themselves warriors with fear and disgust. When a veteran of a war commits a crime, it is blamed on the war and it is explained that war veterans have a tendency to perform criminal acts. Men who do such things may be a war veteran, but they are not a warrior. A warrior is a man who is a leader in his community. He does not beat his wife, abuse his daughters and grandparents. He kills when his own life or that of his family and people are threatened. He kills others when he is at war. To be a warrior a man must have a code of honor, of duty to his country and his people. Killing is the least of it all in being a warrior. Being brutal for gain or just for the hell of it is not being a warrior at all.

I remember when I came back from the Korean War and went up to our local American Legion hall down home in Three Rivers, Live Oak County, Texas. Some of the men asked me how it was in Korea. I told them about some of the combat our unit had been in. I was told by some of those old World War II boys that a man who had been in combat did not talk about killing and dying. It was the first time I had been told that a man was supposed to feel sick at his stomach when he killed his first man and it should make him want to cry. I didn't feel sick the first time I killed a man. He had been killing some of my people and it thrilled the hell out of me to see him go down with a hole in his gizzard from a round out of my old M-1 Garand. I left the Legion Hall, seldom ever discussing combat with anyone who was not a professional soldier again.

Hell, we Regular Army people talk about war and combat all of the time. Go into the mess hall for a cup of coffee and if you see a group of old combat veterans sitting around a table, they are probably talking war. When you go to a veterans' convention, you had better wear your pot and bring an entrenching shovel; with the flying bullets and shrapnel and the shit and blood so deep, you will need them.

I have learned over the years that the reason so many do not want to talk about combat is that there are so few of us who have ever heard a shot fired in anger. Out of the millions who have been in war, only a few have actually knowingly killed someone. That is not unusual and par for modern war. I have done a little hands-on killing. And, if any combat veteran badmouths a man who was not in combat during a war, he should watch his mouth. How do they think we got all that stuff to fight with, and who took care of our hurts but those guys and gals in "the rear with the beer and the gear." I, as a warrior, honor the man who "holds the horses." Now if someone who was not in combat wants to badmouth a combat veteran, shame on him if he is within striking distance of my walking cane. And, I say again, it does not take a combat veteran to be a warrior. That is a misconception that needs to be corrected among we combat veterans.

I am a member of a nationally recognized American Indian warrior society called Vietnam Era Veterans Inter-Tribal Association. I am proud.

Hang tuff.

Major David P. Kutchinski:

One of the major misconceptions civilians have is created by the word *warrior*, They have come to equate the word *soldier* with warrior, and nothing could be further from the truth. A soldier will worry about his career, while a warrior will worry about his mission and the men. The warrior will always focus on these aspects first. A soldier will manage his forces while a warrior will lead his men.

While a soldier is created, a warrior is born. No matter how much training, a warrior can never be created. I have seen many people with exteriors that belie the warrior within. For example, the best man on my SWAT team was an accountant who was a pharmacist by education. Inversely, I have seen Special Forces soldiers who have attended every Special Forces course available, and could bench-press the side of a building. Yet, with all that training, they still were not warriors. The warrior knows no age limits, either. I have met sixty-five-year-old warriors that I would prefer to go into conflict with over some twenty-year-old "wonder soldier."

Major Richard Groller:

A warrior is "not one who goes to war or kills people, but rather one who exhibits integrity in his actions and control over his life."

George Leonard, "The Warrior," *Esquire*, July 1986.

Warriorship is the struggle to separate the possible from the impossible, that which is true from that which is not, in the realms of both the surrounding world and the world within.

In *The Warrior's Edge*, my co-authors and I wrote that the

26

key attributes of warriorship are patience and will. These two attributes above all are the motivating forces at the core of warrior spirit, and the source from which all other attributes emanate. In so doing, we outlined the tenets that shape a warrior's beliefs. These can be restated as:

1. Moral courage—the courage to live life honorably, to stand up and be willing to struggle for what you believe;
2. Willingness to accept risk—taking calculated chances instills confidence and control; being a warrior doesn't mean you always win, but it does mean being prepared to spend your life in the pursuit of what you believe;
3. Devotion to something greater than one's self—be it a religion, a noble cause, a higher ideal, the accomplishment or duty; the extended human family;
4. Decisiveness—the ability to recognize correct action, to take that action, and to accept responsibility for it.

Confucious is quoted saying, "He who conquers himself is the mightiest warrior." Warriorship, then, is a way of life based on a code of honor, that above all is rooted in self-knowledge and self-discipline.

What then is the role of the warrior in society today? It is more than just protector, or guardian, or defender of an ideal, nation, or way of life. The task of the warrior today, above all things, is to be a living role model, one who provides a vision of a pristine way of life. That way of life is empowered by a simple statement: Be, all that you can be. These simple words crystallize the warrior ethic into a challenge, a challenge to transcend the ordinary and become a fully self-actualized human being. It is the task of the warrior to impeccably live this code, to imbue those around him with its spirit, and to mentor those who choose to follow it. By instilling the vision of reality as experienced by the warrior, others may visualize what they, too, can be, and with patience and will can attain. By transcendence of all obstacles blocking the path of self-mastery, the would-be warrior unlocks the protocols of his own mind and ultimately, creates his own reality.

1st Lt. Michelle Miller:

CITIZENS IN UNIFORM

I am an active-duty military officer, but I am not a warrior. I am a veteran of the Persian Gulf War, but I am not a warrior. I am instead—a citizen soldier. Many would regard the distinction as unimportant if they even acknowledged its existence. I perceive integral differences between the two labels. Differences that relate to the very way in which we define our society.

While still deployed in the Persian Gulf, I read an article about the "warrior class." It soon became obvious that the phrase had caught on. In fact, it seemed that the title was applied to the U.S. military in nearly every newspaper or magazine article I read about the Persian Gulf War. I was dismayed. Why? After all, what's in a label? "That which we call a rose by any other name would smell as sweet," wouldn't it? I'm afraid I must disagree with the Shakespearean heroine of *Romeo and Juliet*. Labels are very important. They are the tools we use to classify things in our minds. Therefore, the name we give something colors the way that we think of it. For example, do the nouns child and kid evoke the exact same pictures in your mind? If a mother introduced her son as "My kid, Ryan," would you receive the same impression of her feelings for him if she introduced her son as "My child, Ryan"? the differences various labels engender in the mind are often subtle, but they do exist and they are important.

I take exception to the usage of the title "Warrior Class" on the grounds that the image it conjures of the military is unfavorable, inaccurate, and even dangerous. To support this rather sweeping statement, I'd first like to describe what "warrior class" brings to my mind as opposed to "citizen soldier." It might be helpful for the reader to consider each of these phrases in turn before reading the following paragraphs. In this way, you can decide whether the differences are substantial for you without being influenced by my perception.

Let's begin with the "warrior class." Those words call to my mind a group of people extensively trained in the art and science of warfare. This is the segment of the population that fights its country's military battles. As a class it is a fairly fixed group of people. This implies that they were born to fight and continue in the military service until they die or retire. This brings into my mind the analogy of the Japanese samurai, which many authors use when discussing the American warrior class. The samurai were loyal to their daimyo, a feudal baron. They carried out his orders without questioning their own or the general populace's belief in the correctness of the action. They were mighty, fighting automatons.

When I think of citizen soldiers I see something altogether different. It's that word *citizen*. Webster defines a citizen as "an inhabitant of a city or a town, especially one entitled to the rights and privileges of a freeman . . . , a civilian as distinguished from a specialized servant of the state." Soldiers certainly may be considered specialized servants of the state. But citizen soldiers are also free-thinking members of that state. They are a rare type of soldier—citizens in uniform, who influence the commands they are required to obey by voting to help determine who will issue those commands. Personally, I prefer this image.

Besides being more favorable than "warrior class" the label "citizen soldier" is more accurate. First, because the turnover in the U.S. military is high. We are all volunteers. We were not born into the service. We may depart when our contracts have expired much more easily than one may change the socioeconomic condition into which he is born. Surely this resembles a profession more than a class. In addition, those who would call us a fighting "class" seem to discount the large reserve membership of the U.S. military. In my officer basic course, I learned that 80 percent of the U.S. Army Medical Department is on reserve status. That means that when the call went out in out most recent war, more Army medical staff deployed to the Persian Gulf were reservists than active-duty members. The large reservist participation was certainly not limited to the Army or to the medical profession. Clearly these people are reminiscent of the citizen soldiers who answered their country's first call in 1776. Indeed, many members of today's military work at a civilian job day after day, living a virtually non-military life. It is a relatively small number who make military training their daily business. With the draw down the number will become increasingly small. Of course it can never dwindle completely. Someone must be immediately ready when the need arises. However, the people in this small active-duty pool constantly changes.

What's the big deal? So, those military types might feel better about being called citizens soldiers than members of a warrior class. So, perhaps the former title is more accurate than the latter. So what? What is so scary about the usage of the label "warrior class" isn't how it makes those of us in the military feel, or even the label's lack of accuracy. The frightening thing is the detachment this label fosters among our non-military populace. It is already popular to blame our problems on a shadow, imprecise "them." In fact, these are times of amazingly widespread apathy among Americans. I don't believe that people don't actually care. But the problems of today's world, ranging from overpopulation, to drugs, to nuclear weapons are overwhelming. It is far easier to take a defensive posture, constructing a protective shield of cynicism, than to wield an aggressive sword against so many seemingly insurmountable difficulties.

I contend the carelessly using labels such as "warrior class" gives us one more hiding place from today's problems. That label, specifically, allows Americans to distance themselves from military issues by placing sole responsibility on the "Warrior Class." But every citizen has a stake in our military. Indeed, how we use our military helps define what we are as a society. For example, the question of women in combat has social and moral implications for our entire nation. What military experts have to say is important, but everyone should have an opinion. I do not want to see Americans begin to classify the military as separate from themselves, as a separate class. I do not want Americans to relegate its military to the amorphous "them."

To better convey my point, it is necessary to dissect the rather presumptuous belief underlying this entire discussion. I've assumed that every American adult who is deemed responsible for his actions is also responsible for helping to define and shape his country. What?! But that's why we elect politicians, right? Surely "they" are responsible for making sure our country is what we want it to be, right? Our responsibility ends once we vote, right? We can blame "them" for everything that goes wrong, right? Unfortunately, these attitudes are pervasive in our country. To me they are some of the most frightening imaginable. Because our country is too large for everyone to vote directly on each issue we do have to elect representatives. These elected officials are responsible for carrying out our wishes regarding lawmaking in the United States. But we are all responsible for safeguarding the unprecedented individual freedoms that we enjoy as Americans. It is without doubt an awesome responsibility. However, if we are not willing to make the hard choices that are part of that responsibility then we do not deserve those freedoms. "They" will not protect our freedom. It is our job, and our burden.

How does an ordinary citizen make a difference? Of course, voting is important, but it shouldn't end at the polls. We need to follow up on our elected representatives. We should demand honesty but not expect miracles. Though the vote is meaningful, our individual influence extends far beyond that contribution. After all, laws are only one means of protecting our rights. Of equal significance are our attitudes. What do we expect of ourselves? How do we treat others? The answers to those questions are as consequential in determining the texture of our society as our legal system. For instance, what about freedom of speech? It is guaranteed legally by our Bill of Rights. But what is our attitude toward it? Do we allow other people to voice their opinions even if we don't agree? Or do we try to stop them, either physically or with ridicule? Do we voice our own opinions even if we know others won't agree? These attitudes extend into every facet of our lives. Do our attitudes sponsor awareness of the problems surrounding us? Do they allow us to care? to become involved?

I used to become so distraught with people whose attitudes caused them to bury their heads in the sand, popping up now and then only to complain, that I conceived an idea for mandatory military or community service for every adult U. S.

citizen. I thought it would be beneficial, in that it would force everyone to become aware of and involved in their country. When I thought about it rationally, I realized that the idea is ridiculous. First, it's simply not the American way. The word *mandatory* isn't in our collective vocabulary. Indeed, the idea is antithetical to those freedoms I wish so much to protect. Besides, mandatory military or community service wouldn't necessarily achieve my purpose anyway. You can make a person aware and perhaps force involvement, but you can't pressure a person into caring. It's the strange truth that every American has the right to ignore his country if he so chooses.

That is why I am such a firm believer in educating ourselves and our children about the problems our country and our world faces. After all, it is on our children that the attitudes we cultivate have the most profound effect. Children carry our attitudes with them into the future. Positive attitudes combined with honest education will produce awareness of the world's problems and courage to care. This awareness and caring will in turn lead to involvement. That is the beginning of finding solutions.

When I was home on leave after the war, I visited the elementary school in my hometown. I wanted to clarify what the children had seen of the war on television. But more important, I wanted them to see that I am one of them. I wanted them to know that I'm just another citizen of their hometown, their country, their world. I wanted them to know that it's important they be aware, that it's right for them to care, that it's imperative they become involved in any of many ways. Interacting with those intense, interested children I knew that there are solutions to our problems if we have the courage to find them. We must continue to try, for ourselves as well as our next generation of American citizens, soldiers or not.

Brig. Gen. James Teal, Jr.:

I'm compelled to disagree with the term "warrior class." The picture this brings to my mind's eye does not fit the role of the military in the United States. The Army War College motto is to "Promote peace, not war." This I am comfortable with. We're "fighters" when defending our country or executing the strategy and policy of our nation. "Warrior class" perpetuates a Rambo image that does not sit comfortably with the American public, our legislators, or certainly the news media. I realize the Strategic Air Command likes to refer to their airmen and pilots as warriors. This may be acceptable if, to a group of young military men and women, it aids in developing the esprit de corps desired by every commander. But, to call the personnel of the U.S. military, male & female, "warriors" brings with it aura of hokiness that doesn't lead to trust and respect.

Jim Morris:

Awhile back I was having lunch with a woman who did publicity for one of the major publishing houses. She was marginally interested in my military background, so we started talking about that. After awhile She asked me, "You're not afraid to die, are you?" Her tone of voice was a little awed.

I had to admit that I wasn't. I've been close enough to death a couple of times to know that I can handle it with not a great deal more trepidation than is occasioned by a trip to the dentist. That's one of the rewards. Another, although I'm not sure that this isn't more a philosophical than an emotional reward, is the knowledge that there are no big deals. We all know philosophically that we are a bunch of biped mammals on a medium-sized planet on the outer edge of an obscure galaxy, and that nothing we do has any more significance than flies buzzing in an outhouse, but most people lose track of that in the day-to-day. If you've been a warrior you don't sweat the small stuff, and almost all of it is small stuff. You try to do things well because it's emotionally rewarding to do so, but it really doesn't matter much.

Knowing that you have faced the worst and handled it is alleged to be one of the emotional rewards, but as one becomes older this one proves false. The presumption that facing personal death is the worst is erroneous. It's only maybe third worst. The loss of a child is probably the worst thing, and combat won't prepare you for that; the loss of a major love is probably second, and combat won't help with that either. But having survived it intact can give you strength; there's no question about that.

Major Steve Pope:

THE TECHNOCRAT

As a Signal Officer, I belong to a very specific subspecies of the warrior class: the technocrat. This is assuming that I do not belong to an entirely different species (as is "unflatteringly" mentioned by my combat arms associates from time to time). While I must embody all the basic skills of the class, the soldiers under my command do not normally follow me out of the trench (although I must be prepared for such an event). They do not look to me as the guru, the fount of all knowledge concerning signal matters. The soldiers under my command know more about their specific equipment and how to milk every last watt of transmission power than I could ever hope.

35

The perfect platoon commander would arguably be the best warrior in all skills in the platoon. The perfect signal officer, or any officer of a technical trade, is not necessarily the best in any skill. He must strike a balance between aggressive leadership and group involvement. He must seek advice without detracting from his ability to command. Idiosyncrasies of individuals, perhaps unacceptable or discouraged in combat arms classifications, are tolerated to preserve their specific excellence. These kinds of leadership skills are hard to learn and harder to teach. This, combined with the degree of education required for the technocrat, make it difficult in the extreme to mold or produce the required officer. Once produced, he is vulnerable to recruitment, as those very same skills are more than desirable in other lucrative sectors of society.

It has been my experience with industry that they are looking for individuals who, in addition to a high level of technical knowledge, are charismatic, confident, and above all else, leaders. If the forges of the armed forces do not hammer out such an individual, no organization does. For a warrior to reach the highest levels of expertise as a technocrat, then, he must be able to overcome the seduction of the heady prices industry can and will pay for such a person. He (or she) absolutely must be motivated by the abstract vice materialism.

SIMPLICITY

If modern weaponry continues its trend of increasing capability without a conscious effort toward simplification, the perfect platoon commander will have no choice except to become a technocrat himself. He, too, will face the fact that his soldiers know more about their specific equipment than he does. I do not know why this strikes a dissonant chord. Perhaps because it is one thing for the technocrat to coordinate his resources in relatively sedate surroundings; it is an entirely different matter to seek advice in a fire fight.

Given the amazing breadth of current technologies, it would seem logical to lobby for simple weapons at the soldiers' level. It is arguable that simplicity should be as important as lethality and reliability. Of course, one can always take a point too far, but the principle involved should not be discarded.

Approaching simplicity from a different perspective (and assuming the mantle of responsibility deciding the direction of signals development was mine), my ultimate goal would be the production of a black box with an on/off switch. All the sophisticated technology would be transparent to the commander: he would say "Roger, over" and there would be an air mobile assault. The agile hopping from frequency to frequency, the management of the electronic spectrum, and the selection of transmission means would be magically performed by the innards of the box.

I say this with some trepidation, as such a wonder would sound the end for the Signal Corps as I know it. I must admit, I love what I do for a living and would hate to be the instrument in any form that contributes to the Corps' demise. However, all technocrats must face the difficult task of searching for these solutions to eliminate their own numbers. It is an unfortunate characteristic of organizations, bureaucracies, or institutions that they tend toward self-preservation and perpetuation, or even growth. In my case, I must continually remind myself that one less signaler is one more bayonet on the battlefield.

Dr. Thomas Starke:

CONDITIONING THE WARRIOR'S MIND

Being a commander is a state of mind. It is a way of thinking; it is a set of principles; it is a code of ethics. It is a conditioning to take risks where the consequences of failure are terrible. The state of preparedness, the will to act, the quality of knowledge of the situation, the ability to perceive new threats and new force options, all are empowered by the commander's mind. Peace weakens his belief in warfare values.

The values of peacetime are antithetical to those of warfare. Society requires that war values be recessive in peacetime, else there cannot be peace. When conflict threatens, war values must be switched on, both in the nation, which must support the commander's action, and in the commander, who must believe in his right to act. The commander's ability to act, to strike, and to inflict harm depend on his mental preparedness for warfare. This is most challenging for the military leaders of a nation that reacts to an accelerating external threat. Reaction is balanced between diplomacy and warfare. The decision to strike depends on the military options, the commander's belief in his abilities, and the nation's confidence in its military. Rapid and effective transition to warfare is essential to any nation that intends to defend peace.

Peace is most possible when military leaders are mentally prepared for war.

History repeatedly illustrates that the correct, fast response can change the course of events. Aggression is a continuously reiterated human decision by leaders. Aggression assumes success. Aggressors have doubts. Major initial setbacks and unforeseen events sow confusion in the aggressor's mind. Initial success confirms the aggressor's assumptions and strengthens his determination while silencing his critics. As high-tech weapons make warfare more complex, and at the same time achieve ever-increasing ranges, the transition from peace to war will be faster and more confused. Rapid, determined, and unexpected action will often be pivotal in containing conflicts. Civil leaders will turn to military leaders for options and recommendations. If these leaders have lost the mental edge, they will fail to know and/or act.

A nation seeking to maintain peace cannot afford to be slow, indecisive, or ineffective in its response to aggression.

In the far past, leadership training was accomplished through storytelling. This evolved into formal instruction and war games. However, no training in the classroom could make the leader feel he was really there. Even expensive field exercises with casts of thousands usually failed to submerge the senior leaders in the conflict. A leader's mental conditioning comes from real and relevant experience. In the past, war was the only effective classroom for teaching leaders how to fight wars.

In the past decade, computer, sensor, and simulator technologies have developed to where many warfighting skills can be taught in a virtual environment. Tank gunners who fought in Desert Storm trained with lasers, smoke, and sound effects on MILES computerized gunnery ranges. Pilots and weapons officers are trained in weapons firing sequences by computer. A major part of the cost of each military system is the "trainer," often a computer and a weapons control system. It teaches the system functions and operations. In recent years, units like these trainers/simulators have been combined to enable multi-unit training experiences that operate in the realm of virtual reality. SIMNET is the best example of this. Also, real training exercises have included electronic position tracking, laser hit indicators, and electronic scorekeeping, like at the Army's National Training Center at Fort Irwin, California.

Today leadership training is on the threshold of another change, driven by advances in computer technology. Computers once used a central processor, sequentially executing one instruction after another. Computers are now being built with thousands of processors that simultaneously execute parallel instructions. Succeeding generations of semiconductor memory are born every eighteen months. These developments promise computer systems that are thousands of times more capable and enables a new kind of war classroom, the *warspace*. Here the leader and his staff will be submerged in a conflict generated by a surrounding wall of computers. Their command post will be electronic; they will organize plans by computer, transmit them via satellite, and receive battle status from communications intercepts, overhead satellite photos, and battlefield reports. The real world will be unplugged—they will be interacting with a virtual world, or warspace, created by computers. Architectures and software are being developed to make the warspace so accurate that the commander can not distinguish it from reality.

A complete investment in peace requires preparing the commander's mind for war. In the future, the forward march of computer capability and the development of ever more powerful computer algorithms will arm this virtual reality in which commanders will practice. A nation's ability to defend its interests will be more than a competition of high-tech weaponry. It will be a competition of commander's minds. Commanders mentally prepared for war will seize the transient opportunities and dominate the warspace of the future.

Brig. Gen. George J. Walker:

To survive and prevail, a true warrior must have total integrity and credibility and must care more about the people he commands or leads than he or she cares about themselves.

Lt. Gen. James A. Williams:

Military service dominated my life from the second grade when, following a visit to West Point, I decided that I wanted to go there and become an officer—not so much to become a warrior but to serve in an honorable profession and to defend the nation. West Point turned out to be far more difficult than I had imagined, but the bonds of friendship and professionalism that were forged there formed the basis of my entire career.

For me, the emotional rewards of warriorship involved serving on a team with those you love and trust, sharing a dedication to the common good of the nation, and believing that by serving you helped set an example for those who may follow. "Duty, Honor, Country" are not hollow words but a creed I chose to follow until the day I die.

Throughout life what you do and who you are have a way of haunting you. Leadership, high moral values, consideration for others and trust in what they say are all part of service, whether it be to the nation or to the community. We are known by our deeds, as well as by our misdeeds, and leaders will be judged by those they lead, based upon the quality of the example. That example can be set in official or private life which, in the military, are inexorably connected. There is no room for a double standard. My most deeply held belief is that each of us will be called to judgment for what we have accomplished, but that none of us is perfect; therefore, we must do the best we can with the tools we possess—leading, teaching, guiding, assisting, giving everyone the fairest chance possible to prove themselves in your eyes. Work with the team; make them want to play the game.

Most assuredly there is room for women as warriors in the future. Women have won the right to participate in a broad variety of military specialities, some of which they perform far better than men. Female soldiers may never become members of tank crews or infantry squads or participate in the firing of howitzers, but they can fly and they make superb intelligence officers and specialists. Desert Storm showed how effective women can be. Our military must learn how to utilize them without patronizing them or diminishing their aspirations. Women have proven their ability to operate in unfriendly climates and abysmal conditions and their presence has contributed to, not diminished, the effectiveness of their units.

The American warrior of the future, male or female, will have to be a vastly different person than the heroes we have read about and studied. As the world evolves in the next three decades warfare will also change. Bipolar competition will disappear and global integration will grow, both politically and economically. Competition for resources, food, space, and water will intensify and conflagrations are likely to occur in remote locations and between nations of the Third World. The American warrior must be capable of understanding the causes of these conflagrations and be knowledgeable about the areas in which they are likely to occur. This will require the ability to speak a minimum of two foreign languages and understand world history, geography, and a bit economics. It will also require the ability to use and control others who use increasingly sophisticated weaponry—new tactics, new doctrine, and new concepts of maintenance. An American warrior must be ready to plunge into battle in such regions, but also must be prepared to participate in stability operations aimed at bringing a peaceful end to conflicts before they grow out of control or become a semipermanent part of the local scene. This includes understanding how to operate with coalition partners and international organizations. The government must be willing to fund both undergraduate and graduate education of officers and enlisted personnel at an increased level and fund technical training of the specialists who will make the weapons work. Travel in remote areas should be an adjunct of education not solely for those individuals designated as area specialists.

In the decades ahead the American warrior must be supported with the finest intelligence this country can provide so that our nation can understand developments in regions that at present appear to have little impact on our well-being. This country must improve the efficiency of its vast intelligence operations, eliminating redundancy and needless parochial competition. Long-range investments will be required in both overt and clandestine human intelligence, but the nation's leadership must have the patience for this to bear fruit. Targeting, at best an imprecise art, will not always be accurate or adequate, but the investment must be made. Today's friends may be tomorrow's adversaries or may develop different national interests on key issues and U.S. intelligence must be prepared to spot changes quickly and with a high degree of confidence. This will require both skilled agents in the field and highly competent regional analysts. It will demand skillful evaluation of often skimpy information, identifying weak spots in the data as well as requirements for future collection. Early detection of what today are nontraditional indicators will be required for early warning. Congressional oversight should play a role in this because the Congress represents the people. Yet the Congress cannot afford to grind political axes over the gathering of intelligence. Oversight committees must demand the very best from each dollar invested but should refrain from dictating how or where those dollars should be expended or what management structure should be used in operating the intelligence force.

Micro-management has become particularly vexing in special operations, covert operations, and low-intensity conflict. It is as though both the Executive and the Congress believe this country to be incapable of conducting any of the three forms of warfare. In some cases the record has been poor, usually because of poor planning and the lack of proper expertise. The world of the future could well require deployment of Special Forces and Rangers under the command of the appropriate theater commander for quick and unique operations. Current policies and procedures make this all but impossible to accomplish, thus negating one of the reasons to have such forces. We must streamline procedures and lines of command so as to be prepared for the unexpected. Long lead times are likely to be a thing of the past.

The war in the Persian Gulf, Operation Desert Storm, should typify how wars of the future are to be run. Development of the Joint Chain of Command in which the Commander-in-chief of the theater is responsible to the Chairman of the Joint Chiefs of Staff, who then reports to the President, demonstrated the efficiency of allowing the warriors to plan and to fight in accordance with the policy laid out by the national leadership. Today's communications, and certainly those of the future, permit instant transmittal of orders and responses but should not be used to dictate each and every move on the battlefield. A superbly trained, highly motivated volunteer force, equipped with the best weapons and intelligence available and backed by popular support, can do the job.

Military operations in the future must have the support of the people and military officers must be able to relate to the population, to articulate the goals of the American warrior and his reason for being. The warrior can no longer afford to cast aside the press or public opinion as unimportant or as a troublesome impediment. Without popular support there can be no basis for deployment or employment of the warrior force. Participation and increased dependence upon the Army Reserve and National Guard offer a good avenue for contact with the populace and for building a consensus of support, which should not be overlooked.

Sgt. Maj. J. D. "Rowdy" Yeats:

The one quality that allows a warrior to survive and prevail in his mission is DETERMINATION. One of life's greatest qualities is having the willpower to propel you toward your goals.

A Special Forces candidate must be persistent in his aspirations to become a Green Beret. Once he has obtained his Special Forces qualification, he has demonstrated that he has the capability to persevere and overcome all obstacles placed before him. He has demonstrated tenacity and stamina in the face of excessive physical demands, and has the resolve to endure mental anguish. During training he has demonstrated that he is able to rise above all the torment, and misery, that is part of Special Forces training. But all the hardships of Special Forces training cannot compare to the reality of combat. Those who complete the training have demonstrated that they have the determination to carry through with the mission. That is the spark that can ignite a soldier to step forward and inherit his place as a warrior.

Successful warriors subscribe to an ethic of behavior, a code of honor, and have a sense of duty and common values that they share. But there is an even deeper nature that all professional warriors share.

I believe you can't take someone off the street and train them to become a warrior. Warriors are born and not made. So when you talk about an ethic or behavior I see the intrinsic values of honor, honesty, and integrity, which all warriors have in common. I see a soldier who has a solid base of self-esteem mixed with the awe of combat He adores combat and would pay homage to it if he could.

At the same time he has a reverence for life that demands he carry himself as a professional soldier. In life and death situations his deportment and bearing must always be above reproach: he is a professional soldier. He accepts and doesn't misinterpret the Laws of Land Warfare. It is easy for a leader to play God on the battlefield, but a warrior would never let his position or emotions get in the way of professional soldiering.

Lt. Gen. Richard G. Trefry:

SOLDIERS AND WARRIORS; WARRIORS AND SOLDIERS

To be a practicing member of the military profession is to be a member of one of the most respected of professions. A profession that is, for the right reasons and circumstances, honored and accepted. For other reasons and circumstances, it is a profession that rightfully is despised and rejected.

In the United States, our armed services have both their

origin and their existence framed in and about the constitution. When we embrace the profession of arms, we take an oath "to support and defend the Constitution." Considering the nobility of the Constitution as a political document, our consciences should be at ease concerning our chosen calling. The American military professional has not only defended our country for over two centuries, but has probably contributed as much or more to the general welfare than any of his civilian counterparts. One of the tragedies of the situation is that few people really understand the American professional military ethos.

Our record in defense of freedom and justice, our role in the growth and development of our country (and other countries such as post-WWII Germany and Japan), will stand any test. We have been true to our oath and to the Constitution. (It is interesting to note how few pundits have discovered the depth of abhorrence that the average American military professional holds toward those involved in the despicable actions of My Lai and Iran-Contra, an inherent disgust that far exceeds that of the ordinary citizen.)

Those who have served in the services since World War II have traveled a sine wave of highs and lows in public esteem in the half-century that has been the Cold War. The facts are that probably we have not been as capable as people would like to believe we have been, but most assuredly we are not as incapable as people have made us out to be.

Part of our problem perhaps lies in the way in which we portray ourselves. We seem to be somewhat schizophrenic in assaying what we do and who we are. When we choose to serve in the military profession, we picture ourselves as the personification of the soldier (I use the term generically—it could as easily be sailor, airman, Marine, or coast guardsman). And the solider we visualize is the soldier in literature who is Henry V at

Agincourt, not Don Quixote with the Knight of the Green Overcoat on the road to Madrid. In truth, we see ourselves in all our manifestations. As Wordsworth summed it up:

". . . the happy Warrior? Who is he that every man in arms would wish to be?"

These are wonderful role models, but reality is not literature and if we are not careful, idols become mortals with feet of clay. In an age of cynicism, the unattainable becomes a source of frustration and an excuse for mediocrity. We have to be careful as well as honest with ourselves in describing what we think we are—to ourselves, to each other, and to others who are not military professionals.

In recent years, there has been a proliferation of the use of the word *warrior* among us to describe ourselves. The dictionary has several definitions for *warrior* and *soldier*. Generally speaking, a warrior is "one engaged or experienced in battle," while a soldier is "a man of military skill or experience." The warrior represents only the small portion of the force that is called upon to do the actual fighting. That is why we cheapen both words when either one or both are used out of context. The folly of creating the pseudo-warrior, or the pseudo-soldier, is obvious. I am always suspicious of people who constantly refer to themselves as warriors. Such people manifest a thirst for psychological reinforcement. Even worse, they appear to flaunt their lack of understanding of the true soldierly virtues such as sacrifice, competence, commitment, compassion, and dedication.

To me true soldiers want to make a contribution—they have made a long-term commitment for the common good. (In the dim past, I once heard it said that a professional soldier was in truth a secular Jesuit.) In our Army we take an oath to uphold and defend the Constitution—and that to my mind is more than just a gesture. It is, in fact, a significant commitment not to be taken lightly. It borders on the religious experience of commitment and sacrifice, but because of the power entrusted it also requires a mental, a moral, and a physical discipline that is not found in any other profession. And soldiering is a profession, make no mistake about that.

Barbara Tuchman once gave a lecture at the Army War College on Generalship. Her qualifications were her credentials as a great historian, and particularly her monumental work on Stillwell and the American experience in China. Her thesis was that generalship in combat "requires equal exercise of the physical, intellectual, and moral facilities at the same time [thus it] . . . is the only total human activity."

This is rather an awesome statement. Tuchman restricts the distinction to generalship in combat, which is the warrior role, but then she proceeds to describe all the requirements of the soldier, who out of all of this becomes a warrior. One of the problems of describing yourself as a true warrior is that it has to be a source of frustration, in that over the long haul you just don't get shot at that frequently. (During the periods you are, seconds can be very, very long—and in retrospect, you tend to believe it is an honor you would just have soon forgone.) But you never forget this short window of opportunity to be a warrior. I spent a lifetime career being a soldier so that I would instinctively react to meet the requirements of a warrior during the comparatively short time I have actually been under fire.

What, then, is the attraction of spending all those years as a soldier? Well, most true professional soldiers I have known serve because it is a calling. It is a profession that demands of its practitioners qualities that closely parallel the requirements of religious orders: dedication, belief in service, associations (both personal and professional), integrity, loyalty, submission of self, and all the traits that humankind admires. It is a profession that requires continuous testing of the faculties of self. It is, in fact, a profession that requires constant exposure to physical danger in both peace and war.

If you are a soldier, the chances are extremely good that you will have the opportunity to play the role of warrior. I doubt there has been a single year's group in the Army or a class from West Point through 1990 that has not been shot at somewhere, sometime, or somehow during the history of the republic. That you face those odds is concomitantly exciting and sobering. Exciting for the challenge of "being there" with people you have known and served with for a lifetime, exciting for the challenge of imagining that you may get through it without being hit (it always happens to the other fellow), much less shot at.

And sobering, as you wonder if you have taught your soldiers everything they need to know—physically, mentally, morally—to accomplish the mission without getting hurt. Now there is a challenge! It presupposes that you are a consummate professional who thoroughly knows his business in all its aspects. War is emotional and complicated. It is so dependent on the actions of others, both friend and foe, that no one can ever learn everything about it. And be assured that if you start guessing about these things you guarantee disaster. The mysteries and mystique of war should be sufficient enough challenge for anyone.

If you have enough self-confidence to believe that you understand war as well as or perhaps better than the next fellow, you must then understand that unless you can impart your wisdom to your seniors, peers, and subordinates, you are merely a consumer— a taker but not a giver. Because you must be a teacher. In fact, you must be a *great* teacher if you are to be a great soldier. More than that, you must like to teach, regardless of whether you see yourself as either a warrior or a soldier. Most warriors I have known really did not like to teach.

To be a warrior or a soldier, you must have made the commitment that when you are called upon to fight, you will fight. Fighting is a very, very unnatural act, whether it be on the battlefield or whether you are informing some sub-performer that his performance has left much to be desired. (This is also a form of combat—that's why it isn't done too often.) You have to teach yourself to do *both* of those things, and all the other unpleasant things that go with responsibility.

Incidentally, I constantly hear people talk about "training" people and organizations. This is all right as long as it is in the proper context. If you are trying to impart to someone *how* to do something, that is training. On the other hand, if you are trying to teach someone the *why* of something, then you are educating. In both cases you are teaching. If you are to be either a soldier or a warrior, as well as a trainer or an educator, you are required to be a teacher.

Another capability you must demonstrate to be a soldier or a warrior is to accept change as the natural order of things. The only constant that I have experienced over the years in the Army is continued change. The great soldiers and warriors are truly the catalysts of change. The ability to develop, conceptualize, and innovate is all too rare. The ability to accept and inspire others to accept change—however meaningful, however stupid—is perhaps the true essence of the successful soldier.

Change is inexorable and change is constantly accelerating. In fifty years we have gone from canvas-covered airplanes to ceramic-covered space shuttles and satellites. More than a score of years ago we put men on the moon. The changes of those fifty years in military technology, military sociology, military organizations, and the geopolitical relationships of the world stagger the imagination. While professional soldiers are often accused of a lack of imagination, the ability of soldiers to accept and enjoy change is truly mind-boggling.

If you are to be successful in fighting, teaching, and *leading* the imposition of change, you must also demonstrate an additional quality: you must be articulate. You must be able to write well and speak coherently to have your ideas accepted. And that you have to practice. What is acceptable orally oftentimes is unsatisfactory in print. What is proper in print is sometimes dull in conversation. But the man who can write *and* speak in stirring sentences of simple structure in the English language is a prize to treasure.

I firmly believe that when we limit ourselves to the title of warrior, rather than soldier, we shortchange ourselves. As mentioned earlier, the definition is that warriors fight. On the other hand, soldiers not only fight, but they understand the multitude of internal missions of the Army. I refer to the business of provisioning, sustaining, maintaining, training, organizing, and resourcing the Army. This requires an understanding of combat development, force development, training development, materiel development, mobilization, housekeeping, and the like. Warriors have an insatiable appetite for resources, which they believe are unlimited and that someone else will provide, whereas the soldier by definition must understand the military, economic, and political limits within which the Army must operate. A warrior by definition is almost limited to the role of tactician, whereas a soldier is not only a tactician but also a strategist, which requires a broad background of the fundamentals of strategy. Warriors have a tendency to dismiss or deride formal schooling, and all too often refer to formal schooling as "ticket punching." The soldier understands that formal schooling is continuing education and that continuing education is a hallmark of a professional. The soldier doesn't believe everything is accomplished in a twenty-year career. Soldiers realize that fighting is a young man's game and the contributions of a soldier through experience and formal training reach fruition in a total career, where rank is not incidental, but it doesn't necessarily mean success is spelled G-e-n-e-r-a-l.

Finally, while warriors tend to believe that combat leadership is the be-all and end-all of the military experience, the soldier understands that leadership is the art of persuading people to do things in or out of combat through example, experience, knowledge, competence, demeanor, appearance, probity, integrity, and comity.

The *soldier* knows that command is nothing more than an understanding of the statutory authority provided to soldiers by law to ensure the implacable discipline required on the battlefield. The *warrior* dogmatically insists that men must be led to their deaths because they cannot be managed to the grave, whereas the soldier understands that management is nothing more than the processes by which the requirements of leadership and command are fulfilled. The failure to recognize and understand these simple definitions is what produces the buzzwords and the McNamaras of the world. The true professional soldier is in fact a leader, a commander, and a manager, as well as an articulate warrior.

In almost half a century of soldiering, of being in or associated with the Army as an enlisted soldier, a cadet, an officer, and a retiree, I have had the blessings of a wealth of adventure that no treasure could buy and that only a soldier might experience and understand. I have observed consummate courage, as well as the degradation that results from cowardice both on and off the battlefield. I have accumulated friends military and civilian of every ethnic, religious, and political persuasion. I have been privileged to view the beauties of nature in every season, in every clime all over the globe. It has been my privilege to be present at many instances when history was made, albeit my contribution was minimal. More important, it has been my great reward to believe I have contributed during my lifetime to that experience which has made the United States of America "the last best hope" of mankind, to ensure freedom, justice, and decency for our country during my lifetime. Who could ask for more?

Editors' comment:

Lt. General Trefry's current title is Military Assistant to the President. Obviously, George Bush has many who assist him in evaluating and handling the Commander-in-Chief's military affairs, but this is the person who sits in that East Wing office, near the First Lady's office, down a hallway covered with photos of Barbara Bush and the Bush dogs.

We first met General Trefry in 1991, due to a confluence of circumstances sparked by the fact that General Trefry was using a two-page excerpt from one of our books in his lecture on Leadership. The book, *The Warrior's Edge* (co-written by two contributors to this volume, John Alexander and Richard Groller), sparked comment elsewhere inside the Beltway, but to the authors, the most interesting question was what excerpt Trefry had chosen—and which of us had written it.

So, on a pretext of more serious business, off we went to General Trefry's office to see what we could find out. He showed us not only our excerpt, but where it was placed within the text of the lecture, and other material he was using to illustrate his points. We found ourselves—and our excerpt—to be in excellent company, so far as literary, historical, and intellectual depth and breadth were concerned. Trefry's monographic lecture text not only quoted widely and well, but it happened to include some of our favorite lines from beloved sources. Additionally, he cited his quotations unfailingly, a matter often neglected in Washington, where the theft of intellectual property is endemic by people who respect only the limitations of the classification process where ideas are concerned.

General Trefry, behind his three-star tie clip and his vast mahogany desk, turned out to be an unabashed intellectual, concerned most about the transmission of the heritage of the military professional ethos in this democratic society. Our animated first encounter with him was so full of ideas and their genesis that it resembled more an hour in a Harvard professor's study than a White House meeting.

Of all things gained during that exchange of ideas, the most valuable to us, and something not mentioned in General Trefry's piece here, was that the bureaucracy, like our greater democracy, cannot be faulted for its slow, intransigent nature—and that the checks and balances that are so frustrating when one needs to move quickly through its labrynth are the most necessary limits to its power that keep that power in check.

Personal Commitment

1. What is your most deeply held belief?

2. What single experience has most shaped your current beliefs?

3. How, and why, did you initially enter the service of your country?

4. What has it cost you, in human terms, to gather your military expertise? How do you justify the personal cost? Do you feel that what you've accomplished has been worth the price you've paid? If you had it to do over again, would you join the warrior class?

The commitment of diverse people with widely varying skills to lives of government service is one of the things that keeps our nation strong. Some of our contributors feel passionately about democratic ideals, some about patriotic duty, some about Jeffersonain democracy, some about the Republic, which is why they serve, and some serve for deeper, more personal reasons. For some, this life was the only possible choice. For others, government service was arguably a choice made due to chance or circumstance.

Our first contributor to this section is a Vietnam veteran, a draftee. The Vietnam War will always be an uneasy period in American history for two reasons: first, it was an undeclared, controversial—and subsequently unpopular—war in the eyes of many of the American people; second, for a host of reasons, we performed poorly and our national pride was damaged.

Many of the Vietnam veterans of our acquaintance had similar—negative—reaction's to the Persian Gulf War, which seemed to come more from their own bad experiences in Vietnam than from any external stimulus. This first contribution, written by someone who has spent a much longer time in Vietnam that the eighteen months he toured there, serves to remind us that the people experiencing history often have a very different sense of that history than those who write about it in the clarifying light of hindsight.

The personal commitment of a fighting force to its mission may be the most important factor in a conflict. In peacetime, the desire to serve may be motivated by different factors than in war. Yet the dangers faced by a society in peacetime are as great, if not greater, than those dangers may be in wartime, when passions run high.

In peacetime, it may be more difficult to justify the cost of maintaining readiness, or maintaining vigilance, of maintaining force strength. In wartime, that cost is assessed differently (in terms of life and liberty and right and wrong, rather than in terms of dollars alone), and the debate is on a higher plane.

Personal commitment to the ideals of a society may be the single factor determining the lifespan of that society. Some say that such commitment is harder to maintain in peacetime, some say it is more difficult to maintain in wartime. In this section, we explore the conscious motivations of people who chose to serve their country under widely varying circumstances, and whose definition of that society varies widely as well.

David Drake:

My most deeply held belief is that I am solely and personally responsible for everything I do or choose not to do.

I'm not sure that the incident that caused me to feel that way is going to make sense to anybody else. I'm going to try to explain it.

I was an enlisted interrogator with 1st Squadron of the 11th Cav in about June 1970. The squadron commander, a light colonel, had just rotated out. In the Cav, the squadron XO was the operations officer, the S-3—a major. The S-3 was made acting squadron commander. He wanted the job on a permanent basis, which would have meant promotion to light colonel as well.

The Major was a prick, and he was a really ambitious prick. He put people to making the firebase, the camp, look strack, but what he really wanted was a chance to be a hero and get the promotion. He didn't have much time, because the chances were the brass would find a qualified light colonel any day.

We were operating in the Military Region III, fairly close (I think within 50 klicks) to Di An, HQ for the Cav. The squadron had two helicopters, a Loach for the S-3 and a bigger Huey for the squadron commander. The Major was using the Huey, which mounted a .50-caliber for the starboard door

59

gunner (the crew chief) as well as a lighter M-60 on the port side. Because we were so close to Di An, the helicopters were based there overnight and flew out to the squadron in the morning.

One night, the Major stayed over in Di An with his sergeant major. In the morning, they headed out to the firebase in the Huey. On the way, they spotted three figures in an open field. One of the figures carried an AK-47. They were clearly Viet Cong.

Instead of killing the VC from the air, the Major decided to capture them. He figured *that* would get him his promotion. He announced the citing over the radio and asked for the Cav's Aero-Rifle Platoon [ARP], reconnaissance specialists, to be mounted up in their helicopters. Over the intercom, he ordered his pilot to orbit the VC at low level. He then said to the crew chief, "If that bastard tries to shoot, I want you to blast him!"

While he was speaking, the armed VC emptied his rifle into the Huey before the crew chief could respond. Seventeen of the thirty rounds (maximum) hit the Huey. The first bullet took a chunk out of the crew chief's thigh, putting him out of action. A bullet hit the sergeant major in the throat, killing him within a few seconds. Two rounds stripped the flesh from the Major's left forearm, crippling him for life. Bullets severed the radio leads, cutting the helicopter off from both Di An and the firebase, and punctured the fuel tanks repeatedly.

No one in the bird knew the precise location of the shooting. The pilot headed for the firebase, which was closer than Di An. The Huey pancaked in on the last of its fuel. When it arrived, the acting operations officer called for a medevac, informed Di An of the incident, and ordered the howitzer at the firebase to begin shelling the general area that the pilot indicated.

For the rest of the morning, everybody ran around in circles. Air Force F-100 fighter bombers and the Cav's own Cobra helicopters strafed and rocketed the jungle. There was a lot of shelling. The squadron's tank company made a sweep, and the ARPS were landed. Nobody knew within a five-kilometer radius where the shooting had actually occurred.

Three Vietnamese women were spotted from the air. The ARPs captured them and brought them to the firebase. I was ordered to interrogate them.

We were all in the tent of the HQ company commander. Me; a Vietnamese interpreter named Rocky; a number of officers; a couple of ARPs as guards; and the three women. One was quite young, a teenager. The other two were probably in their thirties; it was hard to tell. They said they'd been digging bamboo shoots. They had crude knives, half-machete, half-trowel. They had no other equipment of any sort. They were scared to death.

Rocky got more and more agitated. He was missing his right index finger. It was supposed to have been shot off by the VC while Rocky was serving in the ARVN, the South Vietnamese army; that was why he was a civilian interpreter now.

The young woman had a little plastic coin purse in her sash. We dumped out the contents. She had a North Vietnam five-piaster note. Rocky lost it. He started screaming at the girl. I couldn't follow what he was saying. He slapped her hard, then slapped the other side of her face. I grabbed him.

The women were all screaming and crying. One of the older women said that the girl's boyfriend was in the ARVN. He'd gotten the bill from a dead North Vietnamese soldier and given it to her. The girl picked up the bill. Tears were streaming down her face. She tore it to pieces, tiny little bits, like she was making confetti with her fingers.

The women were as innocent as my wife back in North Carolina. The just happened to be out digging bamboo shoots in the wrong place—and it probably wasn't anywhere close to where the Major got himself zapped, trying to be a hero. I said we should let them go. They were innocent. Nobody could doubt that.

The head of the Cav's interrogation section, a captain, arrived from Di An all kitted up with a revolver and flack jacket. I think it was the first time he was out in the field. I said we should let the women go. He said no, we couldn't do that, this was all we had to show for the operation. We would turn the prisoners over to the Vietnamese national police.

So we did.

I don't know what happened to the women after that. Based on my knowledge of the national police—the White Mice—I believed that the women would be confined under brutal conditions, perhaps for the remainder of their lives. They were just women digging bamboo shoots for dinner. They wouldn't be able to buy their way free of the White Mice. Twenty years later, the assessment I made on the spot appears to be valid.

A lot of people had to screw up for those women to have their lives ruined, but I was the only human they came in contact with as they went down the tubes. To my captain, they were just statistics, three prisoners to cite against the U.S. casualties (none of whom he knew either) and ordnance expended in a real ratfuck of an operation.

I knew and cared about the women as people, and I didn't do a damn thing to save them. I told myself that what happened wasn't my fault; that I was just a Spec 5 and wasn't responsible. That was a lie.

What I've learned from this over time is that if you live, you're going to have to live with the decisions you make.

Nothing you do is somebody else's fault. I set those women up for a worse time than they've given me, but they give me a bad time whenever I think about them, and I haven't stopped thinking about them yet.

Cpt. Linda A. Gorsuch:

As an MS III cadet in ROTC, I worked at the dedication ceremony for the Vietnam Memorial. My job was to help families find their loved ones' names on the memorial. The sod and sidewalk in front of the memorial had not been fully emplaced, and since it was muddy in front of the memorial, the officials cordoned it off for the ceremony. It got to be quite a job pointing out name after name to the families, who could not approach close enough to find the names themselves. Most of the families brought along scrapbooks and other mementos, which they shared with me. I saw picture after picture of young kids at high school proms with their dates, or proudly showing off their varsity letters—things which I myself only recently had done. Only these kids were dead now. Their families were proud, not bitter, and at least for a few minutes, I got to know the kids they'll never forget.

More than anything, that experience burned into me an understanding of the depth of responsibility I would take on as an officer in the Army. It was then that I most clearly understood what distinguished my chosen career path from that of my peers who would enter the corporate world, or other elements out of government. I realized that I would be responsible for kids much like those whose names are on that wall. I realized that eventually I might have to give orders knowing that those orders would cost other people their lives. This shaped my current belief in the absolute primacy of soldier caring, loyalty, and self-sacrifice as values all warriors must live by.

Major Jim Morris:

Personally I think PTSD [Post Traumatic Stress Disorder] is grief, pure and simple. I lost many friends in Vietnam who were very dear to me, and I have cried many bitter tears since. But even so, the war was the making of me, and yes, *I* would do it again, even if I knew the cost. In fact I did know the cost. I had read *From Here to Eternity* eight times and *Catch-22* six before I graduated from a military high school. All they did was whet my appetite. In many ways the war was terrible, but it was also great fun, and my first experience with not being continually bored.

Lt. Col. Charles L. Rosenfeld:

THE CITIZEN SOLDIER: MINUTEMAN OR MYTH?

When Helen Caroline Critchfield was a little girl she accompanied her cousins to the family plot at the cemetery each Memorial Day to place flags in the holders adorning faded gravestones. It was here she learned the litany of her forefathers, including three who "served in the cause of American independence." From a aged uncle she heard tales of the Grand Army of the Republic and was taught to revere the dusty assemblage of muskets and sabres which had accumulated through the decades—sort of a family testament to the struggle each generation deemed inherent to the rights of a free society.

Helen, at age eleven, would learn of the cost of this struggle, as her older brother, Ross, would return from France—never to completely recover from the effects of German mustard gas.

On the other side of the Atlantic, a young Hungarian tinsmith was conscripted into the army. Handed a Manlicher and taught a few commands in German, the fresh private was rushed off to Slovakia. Two days later, while patrolling along the Save River, a Serbian bullet pierced through both of his knees—ending the military career of Kalman Rosenfeld. Nursed back to health by his sisters in their small village in Transylvania, and encouraged by letters from his older sister who had immigrated to America prior to the war, Kalman's resentment of the Hapsburg autocracy and determination to find a new life grew. The Hungarian Jew who sailed into New York in 1921 didn't know much about American freedom, but he knew the oppression he had left behind. The full horror of that oppression would only be felt in 1945, when he learned that his mother, sisters, and most of his friends and family had become victims of the Nazi Holocaust.

"Carl" Rosenfeld was fifty-three years old when Helen, then forty-one, gave birth to their only child in 1946. Perhaps it was their ages, or possibly their experiences in life, but my parents were both protective and devoted, instilling a keen sense of responsibility and a respect for the lessons of history. I was the sole branch on each of their family trees, but my moral obligation to defend, if necessary, the freedoms that heritage and fate had bestowed on each of them was never questioned. It's hard to say who most influenced my decision to enter military service—the legacy of an unbroken family tradition or the fervent patriotism of a grateful immigrant—such is the spirit of being American.

I never wanted to be a career soldier, but I respected the

belief that the defense of freedom is a basic responsibility of citizenship. The opposing branches of my family tree taught me that freedom has never been without cost, and that it's easier to protect freedom than to obtain it.

My high school class graduated in 1964 into a blue collar world that viewed the war in Vietnam as much as a domestic class struggle as a foreign conflict. Less than 10 percent of my graduating class was college bound, and those of us who were were viewed as draft-dodgers, or worse. As my best friends filed off to the Air Force, Navy, or Marine recruiters in an effort to get better training selections, I went straight from the Registrar's office to ROTC, lest I be perceived as less than patriotic in my neighborhood. Always in love with the romance of flying, and a former member of the Civil Air Patrol, I became an Air Force ROTC cadet.

Although the University of Pittsburgh campus was only six blocks from my neighborhood, it was a whole different world that awaited me as I donned my new uniform for my first ROTC formation. After checking the straightness of my tie and the luster of my shoes, I walked toward the campus. One of the neighbor ladies told me how "handsome" I looked in my uniform, and some kids I knew waved from the windows of my old high school as I passed by. A large lecture class was letting out of the auditorium across from the drill field as I eagerly rushed to my first formation. I walked erect as I proudly passed through the crowd. Suddenly, I was clipped by a long-haired student in faded jeans—the books I held neatly under my left arm sent sprawling across the sidewalk and into the gutter. My intentionally clumsy friend flicked back his hair. "Oops! Don't shoot me!" he smirked, and disappeared into the crowd amid numerous chuckles. As I bent over to pick up my books a girl stepped squarely on my open notebook, muttering "Pig" in a low voice. A rush came over my body; my face flushed. I was simultaneously embarrassed and outraged—my uniform, my books, my country! I gathered what I could recover of my books and dignity and darted across the street toward the refuge of the drill field. A sophomore who witnessed my plight counseled me, "You'll have to learn to avoid crowds. But don't worry, you'll get used to it." I never would.

I became the Color Guard commander the next year, a commitment that led to more than appearances at football games and parades—we also performed funeral ceremonies. Each time I folded a flag over a coffin, my resentment of the continuing taunts and spittle of campus demonstrators intensified. My father, sensing my outrage, put his hands on both my shoulders and said in his soft deep voice, "They don't understand. They can only say these things in a free country—free because brave men keep it that way." Two days late I cried as the Marine color guard folded the flag over Sonny Johnston, my best friend on the Schenley High School swim team. Sonny was a victim of friendly close air support.

With failing eyesight, and a growing desire to really do something, I transferred to Army ROTC at the beginning of my junior year. Officer training in the Army program was more pragmatic—squad and platoon tactics instead of public speaking. It was both exciting and made us apprehensive to think about our rapidly approaching "tour in 'Nam." One of my economics profs asked if anyone in class had personally known anyone killed in Southeast Asia. I was the only one who raised a hand. He guessed that my friend came from a "lower socioeconomic group" and was really the victim of "class warfare." Actually I had lost four friends by that time; in my mind they were really victims of his intellectual arrogance.

As we entered 1968, campus demonstrations grew in size

and hostility. ROTC formations were moved inside a nearby National Guard armory to avoid public view. The draft lottery had the effect of terrorizing those of other than "lower socio-economic classes." Some faces I had seen in the protest crowd were now showing up in ROTC—anything to avoid the draft! I really resented these converts. Perhaps the firs issue I consciously remember changing my opinion on was the draft. I had figured that selective service kept the military services from developing into a professionally elite and potentially dangerous political power. What I was seeing was much worse—an Army that could be injected with apathetic or reluctant officers driven by fear instead of conviction. Soldiers have the right to expect more from their leaders.

Graduation came and went; the other members of my ROTC class were routinely commissioned. In my case, mission priorities dictated my absence—I was given my commissioning oath by the military attaché at the U.S. embassy in Caracas, Venezuela. I have never met another member of my ROTC peer group since.

Following some rather unconventional experiences in South America, I returned to teach aerial photo interpretation at Fort Huachuca, Arizona. What I saw was almost beyond belief—officers, shattered in body and spirit, droning on through their assignment waiting for the inevitable "reduction in force." It seemed to me that the Army was in near terminal condition. I wasn't sure that the Army needed me, and I looked forward to civilian life again, but I felt as though I was abandoning a stricken ship—Vietnam had been a torpedo. I discovered that I really liked teaching, especially Terrain Analysis and Photo Interp. Graduate school and longer hair occupied the next few years. A master's degree in France and a professorship in Canada further removed me from my military past.

A new job offer brought me to Oregon in 1973. A phone call came to my new home, and although I had been out of the military for quite some time, I was asked if I might be interested in becoming an Image Interpretation officer for a nearby National Guard unit flying OV-1 Mohawks. Although I was reluctant to return to the Army I had left behind, my wife reminded me of our new mortgage and tight finances. "After all, it's only one weekend a month," she chided.

The people at the 1042 Military Intelligence Company (Aerial Surveillance) were friendly enough, and they also seemed professional. The aircraft, and even the hangar, were the cleanest I'd ever seen. Nobody guarded the coffee pot— people were genuinely busy; an air of self-confidence was evident. Young soldiers were being trained; old soldiers were learning new skills. I was willing to give this new Army a try.

What I found in the National Guard is perhaps the military that I had been looking for. People with enormous talent, and often impressive civilian positions, willing to dedicate a portion of their lives to their nation and community through a form of service that neighbors or employers may not understand. The missions of the units in which I have served have always been significant—both to the nation's defense and to the security of the communities whose citizens commit their time and energies. Whatever compensation is earned by these soldiers, it is small compared to the dedication and commitment they expend. The cost is even greater to families. As the economic struggle in civilian life had intensified throughout the 1970s and 1980s, so have the demands placed upon the men and women in the military reserves. As a National Guard officer since 1973, I have served in Canada, Japan, Panama, Germany, and Korea—all on a "part-time" basis. The people I've served with in the Guard are second to none—the mix of seasoned experience exemplified by the NCO wearing a CIB, to the young recruit fresh out of high school—they're all soldiers by choice.

As a Visiting Professor at West Point, I was often asked about the "reserve component" by the cadets. I replied that they were a dedicated group of professionals, not at all unfamiliar with the concept of duty, honor, country. I ventured a guess that most of the cadets in my classes would finish their careers as reserve officers and would find challenges and rewards commensurate with their active duty visions. I pointed out that my battalion had one major and one captain who were Academy grads.

The decision not to field reserve component combat forces during Operation Desert Storm was the Army's principal error. With full integration of reserve combat forces into virtually every other service, the Army stood alone in its stubborn resistance to the "citizen soldier." I often wonder if my cadets still believe my appraisal of the reserves.

Remembering the reverence with which the flags were placed upon the grave markers of my revolutionary forefathers, I understand the pride that unites the men and women who serve their country over and above their civilian lives. As the guidon is passed into my hands, I feel my immigrant father bestowing his final charge: "Defend this freedom—it is the best there is."

Stacey Jenkins:

In 1976 I was an Army medic in the 514th Ambulance Company, stationed at Fort Devens in Massachusetts. During the summer of that year, my unit was sent to Germany as part of the

Reforger exercises that are held periodically in Europe. My unit was camped at the Army post outside of Giebelstadt. We were to be split up later and assigned to different units participating in the exercises. Other units camped at our location included the 101st Airborne, their helicopters and fuel dump, and a clearing hospital company. The only women in the encampment area were in our company and the clearing hospital company.

One afternoon we were informed that Army intelligence had received information that French terrorists were allegedly going to attack a US military base, but they didn't know which one. Because of the large number of aircraft and the fuel dump close to the perimeter, our location was considered a probable target. Security was immediately tightened and we were told our personnel would be used as part of perimeter security.

Then came our problem. All the women in our unit and the clearing hospital were rounded up and taken to the post theater. They made us go into the basement and wait until the danger was over.

Without exception, the women were everything from annoyed to furious. We all knew about the U.S. military policies having to do with women in combat positions. Some of us even had occasionally discussed those policies with our friends and our noncoms. But it never occurred to us that those policies could effect us this way.

The people outside in that encampment were our friends, people we worked beside daily, played with, ate with, functioned with as a unit. Our unit included men and women. We felt it was a gross insult and an injustice to us as soldiers to be told we had no right to share whatever the men faced. It drove home the point that no matter what we did, how well we functioned as soldiers, we were defined by someone else's idea of the role of women.

71

I think the night I spent in the basement of that theater was one of the worst in my life. Part of it was the fact that we had no way of knowing what was going on outside. But equally hard was the fact that I was being told that my abilities and skills meant nothing in terms of doing my job, simply because I was a woman. Fortunately, there was no attack, and we returned to our units in the morning. Our protests about what happened fell on deaf ears. Policy being policy, our voices didn't count for much.

I grew up around the military and served for three years in the Army. Over the years I have heard many arguments against women in the military, particularly in frontline positions. Many of these arguments have been worn down through sheer persistence, stubbornness, and lots of patience and work. Yet, many of the old attitudes and prejudices about women in the military remain—that women are the "weaker sex," that they need to be protected. These attitudes stem from problems that women have throughout society.

Women soldiers have been around, openly or in disguise, for centuries. What men can believe in and be willing to fight for, women can, too. Women have had to defend their lives and their homes in the past many times. When they did not succeed, it was not for lack of trying. The bonds formed by those serving together bind women as tightly as they do men. Understanding and functioning in the military requires certain attitudes and attributes that are not exclusively male or female.

Any good officer knows that one of the first things you must learn is that you have to make the most efficient use of all the resources available to you to get the job done. Whatever the "job" is—war games, day-to-day post operations, or actual warfare—utilizing all of your available resources increases your chances of success. Abilities should not be disregarded or discarded because of sex. With the increases in technologically advanced weaponry, arguments against physical capabilities have far less validity than they once did. Ability and need, not sex, should be the determining factors in assigning personnel.

Women have an increasing role in the military, and I believe they will play a large part in the future of the military. As time passes, there will be more female officers in positions to make decisions. I believe one day the U.S. military's "NO women in combat positions" rule will change, as directed by necessity and, I hope, a general change in military attitudes.

Capt. Bill Vlcek:

While there are those who can write of growing up in a small town in Middle America and then joining the service to see the world, I am not such a person. I am a second-generation Air Force officer, a member of that group distinguished with the title "military brat." Born at an Air Force base overseas, I saw B moves before high school graduation. I attended three high schools, including the opportunity for one year at the Lycee Internationale, St. Germain-en-Laye, France, with an exchange program sponsored by the Department of Defense Dependent School System in Europe. With the exception of a brief period after I first began to wear glasses (and gave up the hope of becoming a fighter pilot), I have always wanted to be in the Air Force.

I joined the Air Force because it was what I had known all my life. Where else would I go, what could I do? For four years I've had the profound pleasure of teaching and interacting with college seniors preparing for an assignment or a career in the Air Force. In discussing American national security policy and its development and the concept of professional officership, I have approached, and been approached with, these same questions.

Why do what we do, serving in a nation that until very recently seemed uncaring about its volunteer military? Until a few years ago, one reason to serve in the U.S. military was to protect democracy from communism. Leaving aside the intricate arguments over the actions the United States has taken in an effort to fulfill this simple phrase, it was a commonly expressed reason to join the military; "I want to serve my country." And while the New Russian order retains sufficient capability at this time to remain a threat, the government and much of the country do not see the threat as we once did. Why, then, do I continue to serve in the Air Force?

I continue to serve because I feel it is necessary for a nation to possess a military, and that my small function in the government needs to be done by someone. Given the continued requirement for a military, there is a continued requirement for individuals to dedicate themselves to serve in this military.

The appropriate descriptive phrase here may be one from General Bennie L. Davis: "a profound commitment that transcends personal gain" (*Precommissioning Educational Review*, Fall 1980). General Davis was writing on officership, but I feel his concept is appropriate to all ranks staying in the service beyond their initial enlistment. Military service in a modern democratic society without conscription is not the most rewarding form of employment, in a material sense. Going beyond the material, one is rewarded with a sense of accomplishment in serving the nation at large. In the afterglow of Operation Desert Shield/Storm, the nation recognized some of the sacrifice accompanying military service.

Officership requires honesty, integrity, and dedication as well as a sense of duty to serve the nation. All officers are told this, but they can easily forget these characteristics in the eight-to-five grind of their daily job, especially if the task does not seem to be one expected of a "warrior." When I sat reviewing contractor reports on the development of a new and improved command and control system for the joint community and the Air Force, was I a warrior? While revising lesson plans for the next class of seniors, am I a warrior?

Today's military resembles a spear more than any other instrument of war; those that actually experience combat are the spearhead, only a small portion of the entire spear. Are warriors only those at the head of spear, or may we include those composing the shaft of the spear as well? I wish to present the argument that the shaft is just as important and vital as the tip, and requires the same characteristics as the tip.

The majority of the military serve in support specialties, the shaft of the spear, to ensure that the spearhead comes in contact with the opposition and succeeds in defeating it. Little recognition is offered to the maintainers and logisticians keeping the military provided with munitions, food, spare parts, and functioning equipment. No medals for valor are given to these support troops who work long hours to get the combat equipment prepared for the attack. As the self-deprecating hero states, "I was just doing my job," the same may be said for the people who saw it that the hero could be there to do his job.

While it is true an "army runs on its stomach," the modern Army also runs on gasoline, diesel, JP-4, and MREs. Of the half-million American military serving in the Gulf during Operation Desert Shield/Storm, less than half of them actually heard small arms fire, or the fire of tanks, artillery, or jet fighters. For most, the closest they came to the scene of combat was the firing of a Patriot missile. Yet for the twenty-nine National Guardsmen from Pennsylvania, it was close enough.

They never expected to be near combat, yet became casualties of the conflict—30 percent of the casualties. Were they any less warriors for not expecting to fire guns in anger?

The military of the future will remain such, even as technology provides more accurate and efficient means to disable opponents and destroy targets. The need to maintain this equipment, provide the means to get the combatants to the point of combat and keep them supplied will continue. And the possibility exists that advancing technology will further shrink the size of combat forces.

The future will include smaller military forces for the United States. A smaller, more focused military than anytime since the Korean War. Proposals from the office of the Joint Chiefs of Staff envision a force that will be reactive to world events, rather than our recent forward-deployed structure. This situation will place greater demands upon the combat warriors and the combat-support warriors. An ancient Chinese curse sentences you to "live in interesting times." I look forward with anticipation of the change and possibilities lying before us. I shall strive to contribute my best efforts to my chosen profession, and to recognize the efforts of those who also seek to be warriors.

Brig. Gen. George J. Walker:

I believe that there is no higher calling than to serve in the defense of one's nation. Additionally, I believe that the service must be marked by total integrity and one must be credible.

It cost me quality time with my children, all of whom grew to be good people, due to the strength and love of their mother. I have found it difficult to establish true roots in a community since my retirement, probably because life in the military does not require the establishment of community roots. I believe that the accomplishments were worth the costs, and if I had it to do over again I would do it essentially the same way. Being a warrior has brought great meaning to my life and allowed me to do things for my family that I might not have otherwise been able to accomplish.

I do believe I made a difference in my 35 ½ years of service.

Paul O'Keefe:

The source of my commission in the Army was ROTC. That is the simple answer to "how I entered the service." "Why" would be answered "because I had to—or else enter as an enlisted man." But those answers would be the right answers to the wrong questions. The question takes on a much greater meaning if "service to your country" starts with entering ROTC.

A high school English teacher told our class once that we should get into ROTC in college because we could sign up with a correspondence school in Wisconsin and get great textbooks free. He had found a new compilation of John Dunne poems that had some entries he had never found in other compilations. So when I got to college, I signed up for ROTC.

The correspondence school had become the Armed Forces Institute. It had changed its procedures and now you actually had to take tests and return the texts rather than just sign up, do nothing, and keep the books. I suspect that was my first introduction to erosion of benefits. At least it helped prepare me for the cuts in medical benefits, PX values, morale support programs, and commissary store items.

I didn't much like ROTC. I never was one for classmates or upperclassmen screaming at me to fall in. But when I got to the "decision point" in junior year, where you signed a contract that would put you in the Army as an enlisted man if you dropped out of ROTC later, I signed on. I was not motivated by fears of the draft. I was motivated by the ninety cents a day that would be paid to me for participating. That would cover my transportation costs and buy a sandwich, and that was motivation enough.

Summer camp was a nightmare. Spending hours planning drills seemed like a waste of time. I didn't much like marching around in freezing weather, and I sweated like a pig when marching in temperatures above sixty-five degrees Fahrenheit. It took one lucky break to get me commissioned. The school quota for commissions was 105, as I remember it from my source, Sergeant Ryan. We only had 94 senior cadets. The officer's choice was to either commission me or miss the quota by even more. So, naturally, I was commissioned. That may have been my introduction to the meet-your-quota-or-else syndrome in the Army.

And so I began my career with the Army, which I've lasted in twenty-eight years. When we were putting down our branch selections, I chose to ignore another order. We were told not to include Military Intelligence. Nobody was commissioned in Military Intelligence. But there were some branches I really didn't want. I'm allergic to grass and trees. I had spent four days of summer camp in the hospital with poison ivy. I needed to stay out of the woods. So I put down Military Intelligence and was commissioned in the Corps of Military Intelligence Reserve.

I was the only member of my class to get into Military Intelligence and all of a sudden I felt like I was out of the herd.

Apparently, somebody knew the Corps of Military Intelligence Reserve was going to be enlarged and given status as an active branch. They knew they'd need a lot of officers, and apparently very few people were applying for Military Intelligence. At least they had one volunteer. I suspect it was here that I learned that you could deviate from the norm and still meet with some success in the Army, a lesson that has both cost me and rewarded me over the years.

After sixteen months in school; three years in Italy, two of them in a civilian clothes assignment; Vietnam era promotions and pay raises that made it more economically sound to stay in the Army as a captain than to get out and face the civilian world, I was a lifer. A tour in Vietnam that showed the comradeship, esprit, and selflessness of soldiers doing their best for their country in difficult circumstances crystallized the decision. Finally, some maturation process, which told me that serving the national defense was more rewarding than pursuing a commercial career, kept me with the Army as a civilian employee and active Reservist even after being told my service as an officer was not worthy of promotion.

The "how" of my military career choice was a continuing string of nonchoices that took some fifteen years to lock in. The "why" has been a growing awareness of what counts and doesn't count for me; of what I value; and of what I need for personal growth and where I can do some good.

Dr. Ray Cline:

A belief I have held is that every dictator has his own political agenda. While he may claim that he is ideological, he can adjust and worm around any issue in order to get ahead. All they really want, dictators, is to stay in power.

American democracy is different. We allow people to vote. For several hundred years America has not been very efficient, not very high-style, often rather confused, but we do have what I call a democratic pluralist process. This gives people a chance to say what they believe in and to support their ideas through voting.

I guess I am part of a unique generation. We got out of the university at the end of the 1930s; we went into World War II right after Pearl Harbor, which is where I got involved in intelligence. My first job was breaking the Japanese Navy code, and I went into OSS, which was a very happy experience. I did not anticipate that I would stay around after World War II, but partly because of my interest in writing the history of the war for Eisenhower, by 1949 I had realized that the Cold War was very bitter, very dangerous. The Russians had the military power; they had four million in the military. They could have occupied Western Europe without any trouble, but they were a little leery about it because the Americans had the nuclear weapons that devastated Hiroshima.

A sense of comraderie was built among those of us who were fighting the Cold War, primarily among the World War II generation. The guys I knew felt they had to deal with the Russian threat to the United States, particularly to Western Europe, that it was essential for us to contain the Russians. We wanted to get a network together to explain to people what the cold war dangers were. More important we had to create the intelligence to explain it to our policy makers.

We created a strategy that was peaceful, it would contain the Soviet Union, build up a military counterbalance that would make it impossible for them to occupy Western Europe, and ensure that gradually they might release those countries in Eastern Europe—Poland, Czechoslovakia, Hungary, Bulgaria, and Romania. I never expected it to happen, but it did happen in 1989.

We wrote this paper—in April 1950, Paul Nitze was the chairman for it, and I made a modest intelligence contribution to it. It was called NSC-68, and it was a strategy to contain the Soviet Union and deter them from ever going to war. For a long time I was not sure the strategy would succeed, but we wrote the paper very well. I think the reason NSC-68 created a real American strategy for forty years was because the Korean War began. It was Stalin and Mao and Kim Il-Sung who thought they could squeeze the Americans out of South Korea. Truman responded appropriately against it, as I think most Americans would, and they fought this war. That's when the military power began to build up and when the CIA intelligence community became a powerful force. In fact, we were able to deter the Soviet Union. That is the way the Cold War really began.

The Cold War was a war for American public opinion, and I believe that it often failed. There was a lot of disagreement. There was just this band of intelligence, and state department people who agreed with us. There were Sovietologists who had all been trained by the foreign service. They knew that Russia was a geopolitical danger to us. Most of them thought it wouldn't come to war, but we had to resist Russian aggression. We had to make sure that they wouldn't succeed.

Intelligence is very complicated and human spies are important; the fact that we had this enormous ability to intercept foreign signals was crucial. It was a huge operation, and it still is. The National Security Agency is a crucial area, and since I'd known about signals from 1942, I understood that signals had to be used as part of our research analysis.

One of the great technological intelligence inventions was the U-2 overflight system, and then the overhead reconnaissance system, which is still classified, although everybody knows about it. I was around when we helped develop the U-2.

It flew over Russia for four years, and it was a disaster at the end, but we learned a hell of a lot about the Soviet Union as a result. Jack Kennedy had allowed me to send U-2 overflights into China because there was very little antiaircraft artillery or missiles able to shoot us down. The Chinese government (the Republic of China in Taiwan) flew those planes, and they took full responsibility for it. I set that system up in Taiwan and persuaded Kennedy to do it. The U-2s during the Cuban missile crisis were absolutely indispensable—that's where we found the first missile site with the U2. Actually, what really happened was that once we were able to use all the camera material and put them [cameras] in the huge orbiting objects around the earth, you could discover things that had never been discovered before.

We realized in 1962 when the October missile crisis came around that we had searched practically all of the Soviet Union and found that although Kruschev said he had hundreds of intercontinental missiles, we could only find twenty-five. It was a fake. We had about four times as many because we had tried to catch up during the period of the fake missile gap.

And that's what made it necessary for Kruschev to pull those missiles out of Cuba. It was not what he had in mind at all, and Castro wanted to keep them there. He was willing to have a nuclear war with the United States. Of course Castro didn't know anything about it anyway. He thought the Russians had the military superiority, which was not true.

I recently had a meeting with Fidel Castro and I asked him, "Did you have any idea what the relative military balance of power was between the United States and the Soviet Union?" He said, "No, they convinced me that the Russians had the superiority." I said, "If you had known that, would you have taken the missiles from Cuba? Because that's where everything blew up and it's destroyed you [politically] ever since."

And he said, "I don't think I would have done it if I'd known, but I didn't know anything. The Russians didn't tell us anything and we thought the Russians were superior. We thought they were the wave of the future. We were very enthusiastic about being a socialist camp and all that, and that the Americans were capitalists and were going to go downhill. Later I learned a lot more, but those first few years when I was in office I didn't know much and the Russians never told me anything."

Castro was very bitter when I saw him. He said Kennedy and Khruschev decided what to do and got the missiles out of Cuba. So he's quite accurate when he says he didn't know anything about the military balance of power at that time.

Brig. Gen. James Teal, Jr.:

I volunteered for the Army in June 1951 following two years under the college student deferral program. My deferment from the draft was ending at the end of the school year, so I volunteered in order to get the service branch of choice. The "how" of ending up in the Army was largely a fluke. Several weeks before the summer break a college friend and I visited the Recruiting Command in Atlanta, Georgia, to see what opportunities were available for a volunteer. After spending an entire day with the Army, Navy, Air Force, and Marine Corps recruiters, we were probably more undecided than when we started. Waiting for a bus on a street corner outside the recruiting station, we were discussing our choices when a slim, red-haired Army lieutenant with a big limp overheard our conversation. He invited us to visit him the following morning. We accepted his invitation, and after taking a battery of tests, joined the Army for an organization called the Army Security Agency, with a classified mission. The classified mission hooked us.

Tom Moore:

In 1970, when I graduated from The Citadel as a brand-new second lieutenant, I fully expected orders for Vietnam. But I missed the war by one year.

In the late sixties the war was reaching a crescendo, and hundreds of our alumni were in combat. For Citadel cadets, the possibility of cutting our lives short in Southeast Asia was an ever-present and not too distant possibility. To mask our anxiety, we spoke of the war in a macabre fashion, much like Victorian British officers who drank to "a bloody campaign and a pestilential season."

But after awhile, it was no longer a joke. As the months rolled by, with increasing frequency we would hear the plaintive "Echo Taps" at lights out, each bar of the haunting melody repeated by a second bugler, signifying to the corps of cadets that a Citadel man had died in battle.

Few of us agonized over the loss of our alumni or the morality of the conflict. We considered ourselves warriors—or warriors in training—and we just became more committed. All we cared about was that our country was at war. Vietnam was *our* war, just as our fathers and grandfathers had had theirs. We felt we were expected to keep faith with them, and with our country.

By 1970, the war had entered its "Vietnamization" phase. None of the new Army lieutenants in my class—in the ground combat arms—got ordered to Vietnam. I missed the great event of my generation, which made a lasting imprint on me. For many who stayed behind, as well as for those who went, Vietnam left its indelible mark.

Twenty years later I was determined not to miss the Gulf War as well, feeling that otherwise my life would be incomplete. This time I was going to experience the most profound challenge a man can face, to test myself, to discover unknown depths of character. It was to be the "Mother of Battles," in the words of Saddam Hussein. I believed him. And I believed in the rightness and necessity of stopping him. Now, as an Army Reserve major, I wanted fervently to be there.

Everyone told me it was foolish to volunteer, but I felt deeply—and still do—that the first prerequisite of the warrior is the willingness, even eagerness, to get into the fight. To be abjured above all is the fear of going, for ". . . it is Fear, not Death, that slays."

Friends and family were quick to point out that I was past my prime as a combat soldier. No longer in a troop unit, I was not likely to be called up. Nevertheless, my Reserve active duty had given me valuable experience as staff officer. My OERs were outstanding. And I was something of an expert on the Middle East. It was not unreasonable to think I might be useful to somebody in CENTCOM.

In the end, I failed to get orders to the Gulf, though I pulled every string. My boss, a U.S. Senator, would let me go only for the three or four months of downtime between Senate sessions. CENTCOM would take me only "for the duration," and I had given my word to stick with the Senator. It was a bitter thing to be given a second chance and miss the Great Adventure once again.

Yet life has ways of compensating us in ways we don't expect. By keeping my commitment, I found myself in the front lines of another battle, in its own way even more significant than Desert Storm. If the Mother of Battles was waged in February 1991 in Kuwait and Iraq, then the Father of Battles took place on January 12 in the United States Senate, and I was privileged to be there.

The Senate battle assumed historic proportions as members debated long and hard over authorizing the use of force against Iraq. The President's opponents predicted disaster abroad and dissension at home. They threatened, warned, and inveighed. Then, because they had to, and because they knew a resolute Commander-in Chief would likely proceed with or without their authorization, the senators sounded their uncertain trumpet with a slim four-vote margin. With a muted and qualified blessing in place, Operation Desert Storm was launched.

I couldn't help but ponder: what if the Senate had said no? The President would doubtless have done what he had to do, but at the risk of a major Constitutional confrontation, which could have robbed us of victory. Unity of purpose in war is essential. It doesn't guarantee success on the battlefield, but unity of purpose does filter down to the operational commanders. And lack of unity certainly contributes to failure—as in Vietnam.

It's not hard to imagine how different the Gulf War might have been if Congressional doves had prevailed in January 1991, or if their anti-defense agenda had prevailed throughout the 1970s and 1980s. None of the modern weapons that proved so critical in the Gulf would have been available to our troops. No Patriot missile, no M1 tank, no Bradley, or Apache attack helicopter. Fewer aircraft carrier battle groups—the first forces on the scene to deter Saddam. We would have still been mired in the miserable state of military readiness that characterized the end of the Carter Administration, when Army

Chief-of-Staff "Shy" Meyer complained that we had a "hollow Army."

I vividly remember the controversy during those years over the M1 Abrams tank. But the "white elephant" proved its worth in the desert. Tankers of the 24th Mechanized Infantry Division were very happy with the combat performance of the M1. With its superior fire control and night vision capability, the M1 could acquire and shoot Iraqi armor from a safe standoff distance. On several occasions, enemy rounds hit the M1 without damage, and in several instances the crews did not even know they were hit. No M1s were lost to enemy fire. In the 1st Brigade, only four out of 126 tanks went down for maintenance during the ground campaign. Every one was repaired on the battlefield and continued to fight until the cease-fire. The 2d Brigade lost only two to maintenance. True, it was still a gas guzzler, but it was fast, tough, and lethal.

The Bradley armored fighting vehicle was another defense boondoggle that wasn't supposed to work. But interviews with Iraqi POWs indicate they feared the M2 Bradley of the armored cavalry more than any other U.S. combat vehicle. Its deadly rapid-fire 25-mm cannon and TOW missiles, excellent night operational ability, and armor protection made it a formidable fighting machine, much more than a troop carrier. Yet the Congress terminated the M2 Bradley program in 1989.

There were similar battles in the 1980s over the Patriot missile, which I recall was saved by the junior senator from Indiana, a much-maligned fellow named Dan Quayle, with the help of my boss Malcolm Wallop. The Army Tactical Missile System, ATACMS, which so devastated Iraqi artillery and rear areas, and the Navy's Tomahawk cruise missile all barely survived Congressional attacks.

There was little recollection of Congress's defense record by those observers who complimented the Senate on the loftiness of its Gulf War debate, befitting the world's greatest deliberative body. It was "the Senate's finest hour." Well, perhaps. But it struck me how much like a real battle the exercise had been, bruising and tense. Moreover, it was *the* decisive battle, the only one whose outcome was ever in doubt. No one doubted that we could defeat Iraq. We did not expect such a quick or such a one-sided victory. But once America made up its mind, there was never any question about the final result. The real battle was over making up our mind. Victory had to be won in the realm of politics and ideas before it could be won in the Gulf.

The political battle was a reflection or foreshadowing of the real battle to come. It was the germ, the Platonic dream, the preexistent form, of the real physical battle. Before the act and the consummation, there was the Idea.

The fundamental tenet of Clausewitz, greatly simplified, is that warfare is a form of politics by "other means." To be more precise, by *lethal means*—armed force, organized violence. The Clausewitzian formula is an equation, which like all equations can be reversed. Reversing and balancing the equation yields a simple proposition, but no less important for all that: Politics is a form of warfare, by nonviolent means.

Though we often describe our legislative and policy battles in a loose rhetorical way in the language of warfare, we generally don't approach the contest with the clarity that would focus and invigorate our actions if we truly understood the process as warfare in essence.

Politics is warfare, in essence, because it is a conflict of human mind and will. We seek to impose our will on our adversary, or on the external circumstances of surrounding reality; our enemy seeks to do the same, though through nonviolent means. We employ ideas and information instead of bombs and bullets.

If you grant this basic premise, then it follows that the most successful policy battles in the Congress will be planned and conducted like military campaigns. For example, you would consciously want to consult the nine "Principles of War," which are formally enshrined in our military doctrine. Actually, there should be ten. *Morale* is inexplicably omitted from the military's official list.

Of course, warfare is as much an art as a science and is too complex and dynamic a human activity to be reduced to ten simple principles. Nevertheless, the principles can serve as a useful shorthand guide to political operations, because there is a political analog or application for every one of them. For example, *Offensive* translates to seizing the political *Initiative*. *Mass* in political warfare is *Public Opinion*. *Maneuver*, *Surprise*, and *Morale* are the same when applied in any type of contest, and need no translation.

Just as in a shooting war, the goal in political warfare is to shatter your enemy's *cohesion*, his psychological balance, moral state, or mental equilibrium that allows him to function and respond. Applying the Principles of War helps to achieve this. Other maxims and fundamental concepts also lead to success, such as, the "Strategy of the Indirect Approach," which directs the main blow where the enemy least expects it, upsetting his balance, dislocating him psychologically, disorienting him.

Political combat is much like special operations or insurgency warfare. It is ambiguous, the lines of battle are never clear, opponents and allies shoot suddenly, and the means of combat are limited. The opinion polls and news media, lobbies, and special interest groups with their white papers and policy recommendations are the partisans that harass or support the regular troops.

Obviously, there is a major gap in my comparison—the absence of terror and fear in political combat. I disclaim any absolute equivalence and would not devalue with an invidious comparison the immense bravery and sacrifice of true warriors, who risk life and limb in violent battle and sometimes give their lives. In the safety and comfort of political warfare we risk little compared to warriors on the battlefield—reputations, jobs perhaps. But there is still a mute echo of the battle, an anxiety, an awareness of the high stakes, though nothing like knowing you may be forever maimed or blasted to Kingdom Come. There is the emotional high of conflict, the *Schlachtfreude*: "When the burning moment breaks/And all things else are our of mind,/And only joy of battle takes/Him by the throat and makes him blind." And occasionally there is the thrill of victory.

The 1990s will be a revolutionary decade, a time of immense and dislocating change. The nation's military forces must retain adaptability, flexibility, and the ability to respond rapidly to unforeseen challenges. But these attributes are difficult in a democracy, especially one like ours, saddled with a bloated, self-serving, unaccountable, and largely corrupt Congress that has arrogated to itself the primary role for national security.

There will be more Saddams and Desert Storms. Underlying these future crises will be major defense policy battles. Will we defend our country against ballistic missiles? How deeply will we cut the size of our forces? Will we preserve the warrior ethos, or continue down the pathway of imposing civilian values upon the military, in part to use it as an engine of social change to placate special interest groups? Will true combat—closing with and killing the enemy—remain the responsibility of men; or will we feminize the combat arms and remold the Armed Forces along the lines of total equality and androgyny? These questions will be harder to answer in a time of dramatic flux in the geo-strategic equation, when the massive Soviet threat to the very survival of the United States no longer looms over us.

As a consequence, warriors in the twenty-first century must develop new, undreamed of capabilities and skills. They must have Platonic subtleties of intellect, a better grasp of the conflict of ideas that foreshadows or even determines the structure of real war. They must understand that politics, as an expression of the fundamental laws of human nature, influences the outcome of war as much as the laws of physics. In an imperfect and still menacing world, modern warriors must learn to live with the hard political choices made by the civil authority and, when necessary, defend the bad against the worse. Ultimately it was not force of arms nor lethal technology that shattered the Iraqis, or brought the Soviet Empire crumbling down. It was "the army of unalterable law."

As a foot soldier in this army, I have won a quiet but triumphant satisfaction from the depths of incomparable disappointment. I did not miss the Great Adventure after all. I have served my Day.

Editors' comment:

Tom Moore was, at the time his contribution was written, a legislative assistant for military affairs to Wyoming Senator Malcolm Wallop (R). Moore is also a writer, not only of some memorable Wallop speeches and other nonfiction, but of a novel we hope will soon see print. He has recently been asked to join the White House staff.

We learned a great deal about the legislative process by being Tom's friend throughout budget crises, Desert Storm, and various attempts to shepherd defense-related legislation through Congress. We've seen him despondent about the chances of a program he believed would be killed in conference. We've seen him lead the fight to save the Strategic Defense Initiative. We've talked him down from the highs of legislative combat and cheered him up when backroom political deals were cut that would, in his opinion, weaken the country over time.

We've tried to change U.S. defense policy for the better, together. So we're the same sort of fools, if fools we are.

Tom Moore has been one of our teachers. From him, we've learned to respect a milieu that most people find it easy to disrespect. For us, the most powerful thing about Moore's response is its optimistic reiterations of the basic assumptions that underly our society. Democracy is not a spectator sport, but a participatory exercise; it allows for excellence but inclines to mediocrity, so vigilance and wariness are continually required. Most important, liberty and justice are privileges to be protected, not natural laws that can be taken for granted: *freedom costs*.

If you were worried about "common values" being lost, you can rest easier now. Even in this era of the volunteer soldier, the citizen soldier is alive and well.

Combat

1. What is it like to be in combat?

2. What is the most important thing you learned from your combat experience?

3. What is the relationship of comradeship to success in combat?

4. If you have killed in combat, how did you react the first time? Were your reactions different than what you expected, and if so, how? If you have killed subsequently, where those experiences different than your initial experience? If so, how were they different?

5. How does it feel to see a comrade die in combat? What do you tell yourself when you survive and your friends don't?

6. How do you feel about today's soldiers and U.S. policy on developing forces?

Ritualized combat has been with us for millenia. Combat in today's world is often symbolic. When diplomacy fails, when patience is exhausted, and civilized constraint falls away, real and ferocious combat is too often the result.

The more civilized we become, the more deadly our weapons become. And we must show more restraint as a society and as citizens. Yet, when our government asks us to become another sort of person, to kill a designated enemy, we must find a way to do that with focused purpose. When we do, it changes us.

These contributions are written by those who have chosen to undergo that metamorphosis so that others do not need to make that choice.

Col. John Alexander

Quietly I led a platoon of Cambodian CIDG [Civilian Defense Irregular Group] into an ambush position in the ruins of an old pagoda. They came from the Special Forces camp I commanded, called Ba Xaoi, located in the Seven Mountains area of the Mekong Delta in Vietnam. Though ethnic Cambodians, they resided in Vietnam as the result of the whim and ignorance of European cartographers.

In 1968, this area of the Delta had clear demarcations in areas of conflict. During the daylight we controlled most of the flatlands, while the Viet Cong operated relatively freely on the mountainsides. At night all that changed. We controlled only the area we physically occupied.

Our ambush position was well suited to the mission. The stubbled walls of the disintegrating pagoda offered some protection should a large force be encountered, and it was located near an infiltration route. This was a commonly used route for troops coming out of Cambodia; they crossed the Vinh Tay Canal and then split to the mountains of their choice. Enemy movement could vary in size from a few individuals to rather large units. We were only armed sufficiently to take on a small element.

Within a few hours I was notified that movement had been spotted and a small patrol was coming from the west, heading for the safety of the Nui Ba Tien mountains. The VC had no knowledge that we had ventured into territory they normally dominated at night. It should be noted that the CIDG, mercenaries recruited outside the Vietnamese armed forces, rarely fought at night. The preferred mode of operation was the traditional "walk in the sun," done in a manner that ensured the chance for contact with the enemy was slight. When night operations were conducted, patrols usually went to designated areas, again chosen to keep troops from harm's way.

This night was different. The Cai Wei (I) was along and responsible for choosing the ambush site, and I was carrying one of the two new night scopes, devices that dramatically changed the ability to see and fight at night. The CIDG knew we had something that allowed the Americans to see at night. With few exceptions, they were never permitted to look through the night scope. We didn't want them to know how good it was, the great technological advantage it provided.

As the small VC patrol approached, I scanned the area to see if more VC troops were in the area. Once before I had moved in on a six-man patrol only to find they were the point element of an entire battalion. When we were sure the small patrol was the entire force, the signal was quietly given to orient to the south where they would pass. When I fired the first shot, the ambush would commence.

Carefully I aimed at the lead man and fired. He went down immediately but as the spray of green tracers came from the fallen form I knew he was only wounded. As the entire ambush party opened fire, the remainder of the enemy patrol fell or fled. The CIDG were generally not very good shots and did not have my advantage of being able to see at night. As the AK-47 rounds whizzed by me I experienced a twinge of fear coupled with a determination to quickly end the encounter. The bullets were not too close—close they crack, not whine, as they pass. From prior experience I knew the difference.

As we advanced I could see the man I had wounded attempting to fire again. Again with the aid of night sight, I was able to finish him. This was not my first nor my last kill in combat. Still, over twenty years later, I can remember the incident clearly. Perhaps that is the result of the shoot-out with the fallen soldier.

Death then.

It was almost a game. We kept score. At Ba Xaoi we prided ourselves on having the highest body count of any Special Forces camp in the Delta. Of course, the VC was dehumanized and seen as Dinks, Slopes, and Zips; all names given to describe the opposing force in a manner that made their deaths both acceptable to us yet personally insignificant. But we kept score.

At the time, the concept of dehumanization had no place in our consciousness or lexicon. We were mercenaries. My troops were mercenaries; my American SF advisers were by and large mercenaries; I was a mercenary. The thought that we were there protecting freedom never crossed my mind. In fact, based on the larcenous behavior of my Vietnamese LLDB [Luc Luong Due Biet] counterpart, Major Bull, who was corrupt to the core, I thought we were fighting on the wrong side. This was not based on ideology, but rather the skill and determination of my opponents.

At no time did I ever develop a personal hatred for the enemy. Even when we were engaged in intense firefights, or the night they overran one of my outlying support bases, I did not know anger. They had a job to do and I had a job to do. My mission was to do it better than they did. We did, but given our firepower and technology, it was hardly an even fight.

Death was not a new experience when I came to Vietnam. During a break in my military career I had spent five years as a deputy sheriff in Dade County, Florida. That job had hardened me to gunshots, machete fights, and even child murders. But this was different: I was now doing the killing. It was sanctioned, even rewarded, and, quite frankly, provided a great thrill.

In a way, Vietnam was like living my favorite short story, which I had read as a young boy. It was entitled "The Most Dangerous Game" and was about a renegade big game hunter who would stock his preserve and hunt a cognitively skilled animal: man. Winston Churchill was right. There is nothing as exhilarating as being shot at—and missed.

Projection of an image was important. My nom de guerre was "Assassin 6." It was self-selected, as were many such monikers including Gunfighter, Mal Hombre, and The Blue Max. Six was the standard call sign for a unit commander. Units, too, had such names. I fought with the Phantoms, Apaches, Comanches, and other air elements that brought "Death from Above."

The mercenary twist was clearly present. Over the gate to my camp was a sign, which I had installed, that read, WHAT GOD ABANDONED. It was taken from the "Ode to the Mercenary." The entire line was, "What God abandoned, these defended, and saved the sum of things—for pay."

Not all killing left me unmoved. Two incidents stand out

that touched me then and now. One was the case of a small boy hit by fire from a Cobra gunship. His fatal mistake had been to be with his family in a little traveled free-fire zone when we happened into the area. I had landed with a company of troops and was sweeping the canal, blowing up the small boats these people called home. He and his father ran and were pursued by the gunships. The boy fell, gravely wounded, and was carried back to our location by his dazed father. Looking at the child, probably no more than five years of age, I saw that he was badly injured. To ease his pain I took out a morphine injector and began to give the boy a shot.

It was at that point that the most shocking part of the experience happened. A young staff sergeant, who had previously served with me in Thailand, came up and observed what I was doing. He then said to me, "Why are you doing that? The way I see it, he's just another one of *them*." Even in war I knew there was a major difference between combatants and others, but that sometimes the lines were blurred. Don had mentally crossed another line. It worried me that in a short space of time a major transition had taken place in an outstanding soldier.

The second incident occurred when I lost one of my combat outposts, which had been totally overrun by the VC—or so we thought. The base was isolated from the rest of our area operations, yet was within range of other supporting fires. For some time prior to the attack we received information about a buildup of Viet Cong in the area. The camp sat at the base of Nui Gai, a mountain controlled almost exclusively by Charlie. The exception was a small base on top of the mountain, which we held with the ill-conceived notion that if we occupied the top of the mountain we could somehow control the remainder.

The VC had major camps on the southern slopes and controlled most of the rest. We resupplied by helicopters, which invariably received fire on every trip. At this time the VC had just completed a long training cycle and wanted a substantial victory. In addition, we had recently hurt them, bad, when we caught a battalion crossing into Cambodia at night and were able to get our Cobra gunships to strafe them extensively while they were out in the open.

We knew large elements were in the area. Unknown to us was that an LLDB, Lieutenant Quan, the Vietnamese second in command of my camp, had defected to the Viet Cong. The day of the attack he went to the outpost and took in a number of people, ostensibly new recruits, but in fact they were well-trained, experienced VC. That night there was an attack from outside the camp initiated by the newly trained battalions. While the defenders fought from their well-fortified positions, the "new recruits" slipped from bunker to bunker and shot my troops from behind. They then opened the front gate and allowed the attackers inside.

As the attack began, I was several miles away at Ba Xaoi. Over the radio I was kept apprised of the fight, mostly from patrols outside the camp. When it became clear that the camp was overrun and there were no friendly survivors I reluctantly ordered *Spooky*, the AC-130 gunship that was circling over-head, to pour its massive firepower directly into the camp. The sight and sound of *Spooky, Puff, Specter*—or whatever the names were of the gunships—is truly unforgettable. A gunship sounds like a chainsaw, as spouts of flame reach from the plane partway to the ground, disappearing as the tracers die out. In reality thousands of bullets drench the earth, much like the monsoon rains.

The next morning we gathered sufficient force to enter the camp. In the meantime, Lieutenant Quan and the remaining VC had fled streaming across the nearby border of Cambodia to relative safety. We were not allowed to follow, which instilled a high degree of frustration. At this time overt cross-border operations were frowned upon.

The sight that greeted us was absolute carnage. Everyone was dead—and many things were wrong. Most of the dead were shot from behind. The work of the gunships was evident—the bodies that had been in the open were ripped apart in ways I had never seen before. It was hard to tell that a day before these had been living human beings. The gate was opened from the inside, and other indicators were out of place. Despite the detective work, an overwhelming sense of grief overcame me.

Image was still important, but I was mentally losing it and knew it. When I thought no one was watching I slipped alone into the commo bunker, sat down, and cried. Although they were Cambodians and I didn't know their names, these were my troops and I had failed them. Never before or after would I experience such sadness, frustration, and shock. We later learned of Quan's defection. This led to further shock, because I had believed Lieutenant Quan to be a friend and had, on several occasions, trusted him with my life.

Death later.

Over the more than twenty years since I left Vietnam my view of the death I encountered has changed dramatically. I can only speak from my own experience. Others must speak from theirs. For me death is no longer a game. At times I still think about those I killed. Sometimes it is at a cognitive level, and I rationalize that it was war. My dreams do not allow such rationalization. The experiences take on new forms and often have an unreal quality to them. The situations change and I become the hunted, not the hunter.

The experiences do not fade into oblivion. They are occasionally recalled, in different modes of recollection. Sometimes it is war stories, told with a degree of excitement. These serve to relieve tensions that arise at times. In other settings there is more introspection. On other occasions, one must face the deeper meaning of what has transpired.

My first serious introspection came at a workshop conducted by the world-famous thanatologist, Elisabeth Kubler-Ross. It was a very intense experience in which I first allowed myself to think seriously about my actions in war. More important, I really felt the emotions I had suppressed for several years. Naively, I had thought my combat experiences were cognitively containable and had segmented that part of my life and placed it on a shelf.

The emotional impact was staggering. I was one of the well-integrated returning warriors, a "lifer" for whom the military was a career. Could I now return to combat and kill again? These were very tough questions that I had to carefully think through.

My answer was that I would stay. And should the occasion arise, I would kill again. I now know there is a price I will pay for as long as I live. However, there are clearly circumstances worth the price. Those circumstances vary widely and must be thought through case by case, not hypothetically.

I am not alone, even among the supposedly well-adjusted combat veterans. Years after I returned from Vietnam I attended Command and General Staff College. The classes were comprised of majors and lieutenant colonels, most of whom were combat experienced. In talking with those who had been in close combat, I found many had similar flashbacks and dreams. These were not openly talked about, as we were supposed to be future leaders. One couldn't show any flaws—as competition for promotions was very tight and the slightest defect could end a career. I suspect there are many emotionally hurting officers and senior enlisted men who won't talk for fear of losing their image.

Earlier I mentioned the young boy struck by bullets from one of our Cobra gunships. The tragedy of that scene haunts me yet. I remember the father, helplessly carrying his young son, mortally wounded, looking in desperation for help we could not provide. Shortly, there followed a second father; he, too, carried a small child, but wrapped in a reed mat. From the size of the bundle, the boy could not have been more than two or three. I now have a young son who has just passed those ages. How many times have I quietly wondered, What would I have done if someone had done to Joshua what we did to them?

To be sure, today I still feel there are things for which it is worth fighting, killing and dying—but there must be a reason. To quote Kwai Chang Kane of "Kung Fu" fame, "To take a life does no one honor."

Jim Morris:

The first time I was in combat was like a psychedelic experience. The sound went way down and the colors came up. Time slowed almost to a halt. The other guys opened up on us and a hard charge of adrenaline blew me right into another world. I can still see the guy next to me, firing. I caught the arc of expended shells as they ejected from his weapon, and I could see sunlight on the brass. Couldn't hear a thing. I went right into supertime, feeling like a disembodied spirit. Everything went smooth and fast. It was like that for several firefights, and I began to look for chances to feel like that again. Then I got hit, and the thing that had been my chief pleasure turned into a sour feeling in the pit of the stomach. I could still do my job, but Jesus Christ, I was scared.

To tell the truth, I don't actually know that I ever killed anybody. Most of the time we were just hosing down the jungle. But we killed thirty-four enemy on operations I commanded, and probably some of them were mine, because I was usually the best shot in the bunch. The first time we killed seven in an ambush, at night, I saw this one guy fade from my sights, but whether I who got him or not I couldn't say for sure. It felt like I did, but I can't prove it, and what does it matter anyway?

There was no emotional charge to it at all. It was like taking out the garbage, or maybe a kind of hollow dead feeling.

Then, the next night, I got the shakes, because I realized that if we could do it to them that easily, so could they do it to us.

Sgt. Maj. J. D. "Rowdy" Yeats:

Combat traumatizes your senses. Once you leave the safety of your base camp and conduct movement to the launch site or insertion point, your senses rise to a heightened state of tumult. As insertion time approaches your mind is abuzz with questions. You are continuously second-guessing your operational plan. Within your expanded mind's eye you visualize all the operational data associated with the target area and the enemy's Essential Elements of Information [EEI]. Your mind is processing information at an amazing speed. All of the "what ifs" associated with the mission are gone over again and again. Underlying all your thoughts is that one promise you are always making to yourself "This is the last time. After this mission I'm calling it quits."

Once you step off the Huey, your mind moving at warp speed, your supersensory activities start to convert operational data into "ground time" reality. This is where pre-mission concepts developed from past operations pay off. Past SOG [Special Operations Group] mission and combat experiences have developed your combat intuitive nature and refined your senses to a sharp point.

With your five senses expanded and analyzing each and every piece of data (sound, smells, movement, and the unknown), to function it is imperative that you rely on your intuitive nature. At this accelerated mental rate, every sound, smell, and movement is intensified. For example, one can smell the campfires of the North Vietnamese Army one thousand meters away; one is able to detect the movement of an ant at fifteen meters as it moves across the jungle floor; and the sound or the absence of sound can utterly immobilize you. With your natural mind expanded it is easy to misinterpret natural sounds and movements of the jungle. It's common for a "newbe" to misinterpret these sounds as enemy movement.

Fear of the unknown is the catalyst that expands the senses. It is the unknown that makes your intuitive senses critical to your combat success. You are always asking yourself, "Which direction do I move? Should I stop now for a listen break? Is it time to move over the ridge line? How close should I get to the trail?" Questions that a newbe can't even understand. And these are the simple decisions of pre-contact combat.

Once in contact the combat veteran's intuitive nature is critical to the control of his senses and the situation. It is natural for man to want to run to escape from the dangers of combat. But the success of the operation depends on your ability to control your senses and rely on your intuitive self. A newbe is only worried about himself and his immediate area of influence.

A combat leader is worried not only about his surroundings but about orchestrating those assets that would help them to escape this hell. If you want to survive combat you must learn to control your senses and then utilize them to master your surroundings.

There was a saying in the late sixties-early seventies: "What can they do, send me to Vietnam?!" This was not a question but a statement about life. Within each of us is the desire to live, but for a soldier there is a higher calling that only warriors will or can respond to. Live is precious, but a warrior is willing to lay down his life for the greater good (the mission, a friend, or the cause).

I have learned to be subservient to life. If you know the dangers going into a mission and the remote chance of your survival and still decide to go, then no one can take your life from you—you have already given it to your mission, your friends, or the cause. This same attitude has carried me through life. "What can they do to me, send me to Vietnam?!"

I had no emotional reactions to killing; it was kill or be killed. Violence is part of combat; death is expected. A warrior who has sovereignty over his life doesn't waste emotional energy on the death of an enemy. Even with the death of a comrade, emotional control is maintained until you are out of the operational area. Sure, you regret the death of a fellow warrior, but he died as all warriors want to die. Even the death of an enemy soldier is regretful to a warrior. Warriors respect all other warriors on the battlefield. I have never found a true warrior who fought in Vietnam call a North Vietnamese a "Gook." This shows total disrespect for an enemy warrior. In Vietnam the North Vietnamese were truly respected by those who fought them. *Gook* is a term that REMFs used.

Let us not forget that we as warriors are human! It is very

difficult to hold a friend who is mortally wounded and watch his life be extracted from him. It is the most emotional combat experience a warrior has to face. However, you must control your emotional outrage, for the battle is at hand.

By faith you justify the death of a fellow warrior, for a warrior's true essence is spiritual. I believe that every warrior has a time and place appointed for his death. If a comrade is killed in combat then his appointed time was at hand. Of the several warrior friends I have seen taste death in combat, they all let go of life the same way they lived life. They didn't display amateurish outbursts of fear or tears, nor did they display novice actions in death. They were polished and skilled in dying. They expected and accepted death.

David Drake:

Limited-service conscription has disastrous effects on a fighting force. Drafting people "for the duration," as was done in World War II, is another matter, but I can't imagine that this country will ever again fight a conventional war requiring ten million troops.

Conscription can broaden the base from which troops are drawn and may well raise the average of general and intellectual ability in the fighting force. Members of a limited-service force will never become professional warriors, and the leavening of professionals will be dissolved within the mass.

The worst aspect of a conscript army isn't disaffected troops who think like civilians and therefore believe they should be doing something useful instead of following orders of fools (although that civilian attitude does seriously degrade the effectiveness of a fighting force). Far worse is the expansion of the lower ranks of the officer corps from people who have become officers because they fear they would otherwise be drafted as grunts.

Inept, unprofessional officers do more harm to morale and effectiveness than do their equivalents at the enlisted level. Draftees are usually patriotic even if they're not professional: there are ways at every level of society to avoid military service if it's that important to do so. When the vast bulk of the officers with whom a draftee comes in contact are time-servers—men of modest intellect who lack professional expertise; often men who attempt to conceal their inadequacy by an emphasis on their status as an officer—then the draftee has no reason he can understand to fulfill his military duties. It is to be expected that draftees so ill-led will shirk and turn to drugs.

Inevitably, some of the time-serving lieutenants and captains will decide that the pay and benefits of the military are better than what men of their capacities could achieve in civilian life. Many of them will achieve promotion in the draft-inflated military—and the rot moves higher.

Being a professional warrior is no different than being a professional in any other field. It means doing your job as well as you can do it within the parameters set by outside forces, whatever they may be. No one would dream of drafting laymen to spend two years as lawyers or teachers. Bad as the courts and schools of this country are now, they would become ludicrously worse.

Though I doubt that a lawyer/teacher draft could do more harm than the Vietnam Era draft did to the army into which I was drafted.

Gary O'Neal

Most members of the American armed forces today lack two vital traits that are essential to overcoming an enemy in a foreign environment for extended periods. These traits are self-discipline and psychological stability.

I have fought in two wars, Vietnam and Central America (Nicaragua). The battle against terrorism is still going on. It is an endless battle. That is why the individual soldier has to be a warrior, not an ordinary soldier. The difference is like night and day.

A true warrior does not deal in death, but life itself. It is easy to die, but hard to live. Life is so easily taken away as in everyday living, i.e., car wrecks, health problems, etcetera. In combat the odds of coming back alive is up to the individual warrior.

A soldier is simply a person in uniform with basic skills. The soldier has no warrior heart. They may wear the uniform for their own ego gratification. They say things like, "I am a Green Beret," instead of "I am a member of Special Forces." A soldier lacks the discipline of a warrior. Discipline, as defined by target selection and fire control. Because he lacks discipline a soldier may kill when he does not have to. No matter what their differences, however, the soldier and the warrior are nothing if their country does not support them.

The people of America are the support for these tough, highly trained, and motivated troops. The people who support Special Operations forces must stay as motivated toward the cause as the troops themselves. Without the support of the American people, these troops will not survive.

If we do not stand up in support of these units, we are going to see Soviet tanks on our southern borders. I love what this country stands for. I am willing to die for it, are you? Let us battle the Soviet intervention and kick it dead in the ass. We need to get it out of the United States and the rest of the world. Let us start to build that foundation today.

Many of you said all along that Communism is dead. You said that the Soviets are our friends now. Trust the Communists. Why don't you ask a Soviet immigrant if we should trust the Soviet government? They will tell you, "Hell, NO!" You could ask the citizens of Cambodia, but the Communists killed them all.

We, the people of America, must get off our asses and fight for our freedom elsewhere. If we don't, we will be fighting right here in the United States. If you take into account the drug war, we already are! We MUST give our support to these special warriors WHENEVER they are called. With our support they can accomplish their missions, ranging from dissolving Communist aggression around the world, to combatting narco-terrorism.

The Soviets and the dopers, or their puppets, will come out second because our warriors are the best fighters who ever walked the face of the planet. Their discipline gives them an enhanced awareness of what is important. Devotion to duty, sacrifice for the good of the cause, and a dedication to the principles of freedom are common traits to these men. But these units cannot stay the best unless we train them properly and keep them at a high state of readiness.

We need to put these units in extensive training and let them do their jobs. These units are like the members of a football team who train only to sit on the bench during the game. Let them get out there in the game. That is what we are paying them for! These warriors are willing to give their lives in defense of that freedom for which our forefathers fought so hard.

Only with a warrior spirit and self-discipline can a man persist in the path of the warrior. The true warrior must master the arts of camouflage, concealment, and movement. The proper psychological integration for these arts is essential for mastering fighting techniques, with or without a weapon. Mastering hand-to-hand techniques intensifies and enhances physical, mental, and spiritual development. This inner balance allows the serious student to grow into an astonishing fighting machine.

The American warrior's fierce fighting spirit and highly developed mind and body are exemplified in the warrior's code of ethics:

1. Loyalty to God.
2. Loyalty to country.
3. Loyalty to parents.
4. Trust in friends and family.
5. Never retreat from the enemy.
6. Never take a life without cause. If your opponent draws blood, you break bones. If they break bones, you exterminate them.

The individual warrior needs a foundation on which to build. Building a mountain of rock on a foundation of sand is like building the individual warrior. The foundation is necessary to support the mountain of knowledge that the individual warrior in today's armed forces needs more than ever. Today, we have the greatest responsibility ever placed on the American warrior because of the world situation. Communist insurgencies and terrorism occur everyday. This is our way today, to battle this threat.

The next war we fight will probably not be a high-intensity nuclear war. The wars of the future will be like Vietnam,

110

Central America, and the Middle East. If there is another war like WWI or WWII, it will be the last. The reason is that nobody likes to lose. The loser will initiate the nuclear war. Then everybody will lose. Read your history books, then closely follow the world situation.

We need more realistic training because the way you train in peacetime is the way you are going to fight in actual combat. After nineteen years of training and teaching this is what we need for the foundation in today's armed forces. Training in hand-to-hand combat, sentry stalking, and silent kill are needed. Martial arts or karate do not address the problem. Only hand-to-hand combat. There are thousands of self-defense or martial arts in the world today and they all claim that their art is the best. You can go to any store and find hundreds of books on the self-defense and martial arts. They all convey the same theme: "the secret art of self-defense." They are all WRONG.

There are no secrets in hand-to-hand. It is all up to your imagination. It is plain and simple: life or death.

Today, everyone thinks we do not need hand-to-hand combat. They feel we can rely on modern technology and the weapons it has spawned. Weapons do not engage in the fighting, people do. Weapons are only the extension of the warrior; the warrior is the basic weapon. If we did away with the warrior, weapons would have no purpose.

Knowledge and capabilities in hand-to-hand gives the warrior a concrete foundation upon which he can build. The use of modern weapons technology provides the individual with a platform of sand. The warrior must have the confidence in themselves to battle without modern technology. It might not always be there. The ammunition might run out. The weapons may break down. Hand-to-hand combat training will give him the ability to continue to fight and survive.

The essential ingredients required for the proper development of the serious hand-to-hand devotee are available. You can find them within the disciplines of hand-to-hand combat, sentry stalking, and silent kill training. Be sure when you study these that the primary focus is on survival in combat. The physical and mental discipline will separate the warriors from the soldiers. In most situations, we mentally and physically limit ourselves by placing restrictions on our minds and bodies. This blocks our creative imaginations. We must develop the proper mental attitude for battle. Knowledge and a true heart can help you survive. Sheer willpower, and a sense of justice and fair play, will also help.

However, in combat situations when the emphasis is on survival, the warrior must be able to commit himself to the practical application of all acquired knowledge and skills. His proper actions and reactions are swift and decisive. These skills must become second nature, so once committed, the warrior can direct the flow of events. Thus bringing the situation to a victorious conclusion.

1st Lt. Clifford R. Fagan

I remember sitting in a crowded classroom at Fort Benning, "Home of the Infantry," when a young lieutenant would ask that inevitable question: "Does the Geneva Conventions really serve any purpose when the only countries we are likely to fight ignore them?" We enjoyed watching the instructor squirm to defend ideas he wasn't sure he believed. For years we considered it a favorite topic. At least until we got a gut full of death in Panama and the Persian Gulf.

I had a bit of an edge in understanding these things having

112

friends who served in Vietnam and eight years of prior service, but I admit I had serious doubts whether the Geneva Conventions served any purpose against North Koreans, Vietnamese, Chinese, or Soviets. Ranger school didn't improve this much. Although the Ranger instructors did a wonderful job teaching small unit operations and never recommended breaking Geneva Conventions, they prefaced each type of patrol with the reasons why we didn't want to take any prisoners.

Their methods did not include shooting people after their capture, but they made certain we understood the ethical questions we would face if we ever let an enemy get close enough to surrender while operating behind enemy lines. Taking prisoners could get all our soldiers either killed or captured, not to mention causing the mission to fail. It seemed that most of those pesky prisoners didn't feel obliged to move swiftly or silently after capture. The solution was simple: avoid all contact or make sure they never got a chance to surrender.

Except for reconnaissance missions, this second option was generally necessary. Approaching an enemy while they were still breathing is dangerous, so after the first onslaught from claymores and automatic weapons fire, individuals were each targeted with additional rounds and grenades to make sure they were dead. After that we were to wait and listen for the moans of the wounded and target that vicinity with more rounds and grenades until it stopped. At that point, we were told, tear gas was sometimes used to make sure none of them were playing possum, but officially we had to get permission from the President to use tear gas, so we were to use our own judgment. If we suspected someone of playing possum, we were to put enough gunfire and grenades on them to ensure their death before we approached. The point of all this was that we had to search the bodies for secret code books or map locations. A wounded soldier might come up with a pistol, a grenade, or worst of all, a white flag when we got close to him.

I kept waiting to see if there was any kind of Ranger patrol where prisoners would be acceptable. After the final patrol class started out with the standard warning against taking prisoners, I asked the instructor about it. He honestly tried to think of one and couldn't.

It is any wonder that most soldiers are cold and emotionally distant for about three months after sleep deprivation brain-washing and shock troop training in Ranger school? I have deep respect for the quality of the training I received there and for every instructor I met. This is the best method they have devised to teach tactics, weed out the weak and unstable, and prepare cold-blooded killers, capable of killing without hesitation, in only three months time.

These are all critical survival skills in a war zone, and although Rangers are hard to deal with in peacetime, they stand a much better chance than most of finishing missions both alive and sane. I'll never again have to question my ability to do whatever is necessary. It's true that my marriage took a severe turn for the worse afterward, but it takes most men about three months before they open up enough to feel normal emotions again.

All in all, I feel that learning to turn the volume control to my emotions up or down at will strengthened me tremendously. It's true that some men never did get their emotions turned back on and cracked up eventually, but those are the fortunes of war.

I looked at the question of the Geneva Conventions and "ethics of war" a little differently now that I realize what effect such ruthless methods have on the mind of the soldier employing them. I listen to the debates between young lieutenants now from a somewhat different perspective. I also notice that the old sergeant majors and Vietnam veterans just shake their heads and walk away.

I finally started asking some of our Vietnam veterans what they thought about the Geneva Conventions. The general response was something on the order of "You gotta have some kinda rules or else the troops get wild and you can't handle them!" I found out about troops without correct discipline "fragging" their lieutenants. It seems that platoon leaders who made too many mistakes or volunteered for too many missions were considered a threat to their soldiers lives. Their soldiers were accustomed to direct solutions for lethal threats, like rolling a grenade under the officer's cot. If the soldiers were used to destroying their enemies in a ruthless, amoral, and lawless manner, what difference did it really make if the enemy was wearing the same uniform or not?

Let's put ethics and morality aside for a minute and just look at hand practical facts. Ethics usually aren't at the top of anybody's mind when they are being shot at, American soldiers don't fight for Mom and apple pie, their girlfriend, their President, the Constitution, or an abstract concept like free-dom. They are too busy killing and dying to worry about anything they haven't seen or touched in the last ten minutes. Those things might get them on the plane or landing craft, but when they go out the door, so do the high-minded concepts! Private Joe Snuffy usually doesn't understand or even know why he's attacking or defending some hill. We teach "keeping the troops informed" and "commander intent," but it doesn't always translate into a reality on the battlefield. I'm not really sure Snuffy would care too much even if he did, unless it could be translated into the lives of someone he knew and cared about.

Private Joe Snuffy fights because if he doesn't, his buddy Private Brown next to him is going to die. American soldiers will fight and die for the soldier in the hole next to them. That's what makes American soldiers so tough to beat and makes their enemies terrified of the "crazy Americans." We don't have a big problem with soldiers running in panic or refusing to face danger. What we do have problems with are alcoholism, drug abuse, psychosis, and psychopathic cripples after the battles are done.

Most of these casualties come from units where they got so fed up with the Viet Cong ruthlessness killing off their buddies they threw out the rule book. Not all massacres were as obvious as MyLai. Veterans often tell me stories about Navy SEAL teams putting ground glass in the rice bins of villages that supported and protected the Viet Cong to make sure they couldn't help Charlie kill any more Americans. In a few days the village would be nothing but corpses, from the oldest man to the youngest child. Viet Cong prisoners were sometimes interrogated by pushing them out of a helicopter at high altitudes, one by one, until someone got talkative. Sailors would tell me about keeping civilian boat people from swarming onboard ships with flame-throwers, burning any man, woman, or child who tried to board. Is it any wonder many of our survivors are emotional cripples?

Whose fault is it? There's no point blaming the incredible, psychopathic ruthlessness of the Viet Cong. Even if they did force our soldiers to shoot bomb-carrying children, we can't control what others do. Our leaders have a responsibility to complete missions with a minimum of casualties, mentally as well as physically.

It should be obvious that a culture that forces children to memorize verses such as "Thou shalt not kill" and then drops them in the jungle with a few weeks of obsolete training does not prepare them for the realities of war. Our training today is vastly superior to what soldiers received during the rapid buildup of the Vietnam era, but it will never be enough. It is our responsibility as leaders to understand what our soldiers will need to stay as sane as possible while slaughtering their fellow man.

It would be incredibly sane if our public recognized a few realities about war and our cultural training and values. It's terribly confusing to teach goals that are impossible to meet, especially when theologians insist that the Hebrew source of the commandment is correctly translated "Thou shalt not murder." Something needs to be done to help soldiers perceive themselves as staying within the guidelines of moral decency when they do the things we order them to do. If they return from defending their country to find people calling them baby-killers and spitting on them, it is pretty tough to retain much of a self-image. Some Vietnam veterans not only turned to drugs or alcohol but continued killing for a living here in the United States. If they sometimes had no rules in Vietnam other than "Don't get caught," why not make a good living the same way here?

The Geneva Conventions lend an air of moral decency. They establish limits and guidelines for "moral" conduct of war and humane treatment of prisoners in a way that does not significantly lessen a unit's fighting abilities. The rules are difficult to follow sometimes, but never impossible, and lend enough of an air of respectability to the bloody business of war to allow a soldier to think of himself as honorable and tell himself: "I don't kill when I want to, only to stay alive."

Whether you or I believe any of this is immaterial. It gives a man struggling in a sea of insanity something to cling to. He can still consider himself "good" and consider the people who don't fight by the rules "bad." What's more, he won't have to worry about whether or not he might kill a fellow soldier, a rude civilian, or someone who just plain pisses him off when he gets back home.

My observations and experiences in our recent wars and skirmishes indicate that strict enforcement of the Geneva Conventions and moral support from civilians at home did wonders for young men's abilities to come back sane. Even the Korean War and World War II didn't produce the horrible psychological damage that our handling of the Vietnam War produced in the poor men and boys from whom we had already demanded so much.

The Geneva Conventions are less to protect the conquered, who can't enforce them anyway, than to protect the conqueror from winning the war and losing sanity in the process.

SFC Ronald E. McGuire:

Today, I still think about the last year of the Vietnam War.

I was stationed in Thailand, at the Royal Thai Air Force Base at Udorn. As the last hour of a dayshift came to a close we received word that the air base eight miles down the road was hit by sappers. Satchel charges were carried right onto the flight line by two CTs [Communist Terrorists]. These agents of the North Vietnamese were shot and killed taking to Buddah the knowledge of other CTS and their planned activities. Would we at the 7th RRFS [Radio Research Field Station] be attacked as well?

The commander called out the QRF [Quick Reaction Force] squad and I left the maintenance shop thirty minutes early. I

joined this small band of seasoned chair sitters, brought together less than four months earlier, to assist the "local national" guard force defend our small outpost.

Those of us who quickly gathered at the gate of the arms
room patiently waited until the holder of the key was found.
Weapons (M-16s, .45s, and our two illumination-only mortars) and ammunition were then issued. As the other mortar
crew members and I lay in the tubes so we could illuminate the
large fields at both ends of the post, the QRF NCOIC began
positioning personnel in the small perimeter bunkers on the
north end of the post. The local national guard force, still
manning all the guard towers, sent additional personnel to the
bunkers on the south end of the post. The surrounding rice
fields, wooded areas, and a busy north-south highway provided
CTs with many avenues of approach.

The setup and personnel placement used up most of the
remaining daylight, and with the fading light came monsoon
rains. Not only would the night's darkness hamper early detection of any advancing CTs, but the sheets of rain now coming
down would restrict our vision to near zero.

Through the night, two-hour shifts with the mortars and in
the bunkers allowed each of us ample time to reflect on
whatever we chose. I lapsed into my own thought world,
briefly thinking of home, Mom, and my brother and sisters.
The current situation started to invade these refreshing
thoughts and I began to think about how I had gotten myself
into this situation of sitting in the rain and mud waiting for an
unknown event that may end my life. Hadn't I joined the Army
Security Agency to stay out of combat?

During my eight years in the military I hadn't spent any time
with nor time around combat units. My learning process about
squad tactics, fire team maneuvers, mortar team positions and

responsibilities, and general defense of a military installation began only during the last two or three months.

The arrival of a new NCO three or four months earlier was the beginning of this band of defenders. The new NCO and his equally new lieutenant viewed the post perimeter defense while jogging together. After further discussion about defensive inadequacies, work started on the QRF. The call went out for volunteers to staff the new defensive organization. The first people to join held meetings to discuss ideas. What would we name the group? What weapons were available and what additional weapons were needed? Most of us had not seen an FM [Field Manual] since Basic or Air and were only familiar with the M-16 rifle.

The procurement of the necessary FMs and additional weapons were first on the list. Since we were a passive noncombat unit, we had but a few (100 or so) M-16s and enough .45s for each officer. The mortars we obtained and used for nighttime illumination were not on our TDA.

The weeks required to round up our needed materials were spent studying the FMs the average infantryman knows like the back of his hand. Some team members learned quickly how to set up a perimeter defense and advance a fire team. Others of us learned about the weapon that would provide us with nighttime illumination. Most of the people appeared genuinely interested in the top performance of our little band. To the majority of us noncombatants, protection of the field station and the personnel stationed there became our highest priority.

As the squad proceeded through tactical training, fire maneuvers, and additional training with the M-16, I often wondered, Were we really prepared to do the job of perimeter defense? Was our training enough to stop an all-out attack by the seasoned professional CTs that may be coming our way?

Now my thoughts were interrupted by a call from team members. It was our turn to provide relief to the guys out in the rain. As we scurried along between buildings to our designated post a chill came over me. Were the CTs able to see us? Could their snipers pick us off during our movements? Hurry along, you guys, let's get down behind the sandbags.

Staring into the night with rain blowing in your face is a lonely feeling you must experience, for it is not describable to anyone. The English language as taught in the schools of my youth do not contain the words necessary for me to convey the feeling I had that night. Don't retreat into your thoughts, Ronn, I told myself repeatedly. Mental alertness is the beginning of survival: keep your edge.

Instead of the two hours I was actually on perimeter defense, my mind told me several days had passed. Who robbed us of our daylight?

At the end of my first guard shift I dried off some and drifted back to my world. How many hours or days of my off-duty time had I spent learning the skills I might need tonight?

As additional weapons and training ammunition arrived we began the process of learning or relearning how to properly fire the M-16. Sustained one-minute cover fire: did I really make that one twenty-round clip last a whole minute? One- and two-hundred-yard accuracy shots: Was that really my bullet that hit the target? Familiarization fire (practice once a year) had not kept my skill with a rifle as sharp as I thought.

Sitting in the dim light of the training NCO's office (our command post) I asked myself about the team members I had come to know. Did they really understand all the lessons and tactics we had learned these past months? I was sure they were wondering the same thing about me.

In small groups we had practiced squad tactics under the

heat of the Thailand sun, never realizing we would put the training to use at night in monsoon rains. Were we all crazy for becoming involved with the QRF? Did we all have a death wish? Surely each of us had taken a personal accounting prior to tonight. Maybe not all—I was taking mine now.

A restless sleep overcame me as I propped myself against the wall. Maybe this is the time I started to forget my dreams. That night's dreams were not worth remembering.

A voice woke me, two more perimeter guard tours were mine to serve that night.

The rains continued off and on during the night. The dawn drove the rains and the ugly clouds away. The bright orange ball rising in the east helped clear the cobwebs from my brain. The short restless naps I had taken when breaks came left my mind cluttered with fond memories along with the fears of what could have happened during the night.

Now we faced one more check, the northern perimeter sweep to assure ourselves and our command group that no CTs had penetrated our defenses. Adequate sunlight allowed us to see all our outer boundaries from one spot. The lieutenant pulled all personnel in to the command post and issued the new objective. Sweep the north end of the post while the local national guards swept the south end of the post.

Spreading out to perform the sweep the more experienced interlaced themselves with the newer members of the QRF. Constant reminders to "stay alert" drifted on the morning winds from member to member. Older helping younger/ newer as we waded through fields of wet grass and into puddles and pools of trapped water. Pesky bugs of all types attacked us from all sides.

A slow methodical search allowed us to look in every possible hiding place as we wheeled the squad around the corners and straight stretches of the northern end of the post. As we approached the antenna field apprehension grew among the squad members. One hundred and forty-four antenna bases had to be individually searched. The closed bases are large enough to provide a perfect hiding place for a person or a satchel charge.

It took us two hours to finish the sweep. Without benefit of a formation the lieutenant dismissed us. As a mortar crew member I had to help disassemble the mortars for turn-in. I also cleaned the mortar tubes and my M-16 and turned them into the arms room.

Walking back to the barracks with a couple of guys I tried to make light of the past night's events. We told a couple of jokes and laughed, even though the jokes were not that funny. I know I was deep in thought about how close I had come to returning to the United States in a body bag. I was glad I had made it through the night. I remember thinking, this must be the feeling every man and woman in Vietnam has when they wake up each and every day.

I thought about the job of the QRF over the next week or two. Had we spent our training time learning the right things? Had the squad members learned all of the tasks properly? Were all of them, was I, willing to pull the trigger if the time had come on that rainy night? I had never before consciously put my life into the hands of others in the manner I had that night.

I learned from brief discussion in the following weeks that all participants had gained a new appreciation of the combat soldier. The night had brought separate army factions together in spirit. A few noncombatants understood the fears of the combat soldier even though no shots were ever fired.

Editors' comment:

Ron McGuire talks about what it does to a "seasoned chair sitter" to finally see combat. Without apology, McGuire explains that he joined the Army Security Agency to stay out of combat. Many of us may have forgotten the ethos of the sixties, the order of the day for the sixties soldier: stay alive. McGuire reminds us that not all men looked at all wars as a test of manhood, of technology, or of national might. The Vietnam War, in particular, was a war that caused many to consider its only important test to be a pass/fail exercise—to fail was to come home in a body bag.

McGuire was a member of a "passive noncombat unit"— and proud of it. He ranks survival as a primary goal, as so many have done through the ages—those who have fought and lived to tell of so many wars. His cathartic piece provides a glimpse of living memory, a window into an experience that has stayed fresh through so many intervening years. The Vietnam experience, as it is called, may be closer to McGuire's, on average, than to many other views expressed in this volume. We're glad to have it. We knew we needed it. We couldn't ask for it. We simply had to wait and hope that the law of averages would provide it.

The World

1. How does media coverage by the press, or lack of it, affect military operations?

2. U.S. forces may increasingly be called upon to restore order, make or keep peace abroad. It is said that an occupying force can seldom defeat a hostile indigenous populace. Is this proposition historically true, and how does it affect the missions we will be facing in the third world as the world's power blocs realign?

We're not alone anymore, whatever the protectionists and isolationists may wish. Our economy is tied to the global economy. Our industries, geared to global markets, suffer when oil flow is disrupted or other nations won't freely trade our goods. Our stores are full of imported products and their stores are full of our products.

Their armies were full of our weapons, and their borders were full of our soldiers, sailors, and pilots, until the bipolar world came to an abrupt end in 1989. Now we are trying to grapple with a build-down not only of nuclear and conventional military force, but of military production, which may be economically disastrous for all the countries of the Western world. Nowhere is U.S. economic interdependence on offshore factors clearer than in the current difficulties of U.S. "defense conversion." With the end of bipolar stability came the chaos that is currently reflected in our economy, and it may continue to effect our economic stability for years to come.

Why is this happening? The United States and the Soviets both stopped supporting their client states. Sometimes abruptly, sometimes less so; small wars around the globe that were supported by the superpowers were brought to an end. Clients for U.S. military production have diminished and, despite the transient Gulf War boom, will keep diminishing unless some offshore military threat materializes.

The era of the dueling superpowers may have reached its end. By one military measure, the United States already stands alone, the single superpower, leader of the world. But can we prosper without our former partner, the once-great Soviet Union, to goad us to action? One-quarter of our Gross National Product was Cold War related.

No great society before us has ever managed to maintain its power without projecting force. Throughout history, societies have gone into decline once their enemies were vanquished. If we cannot learn to prosper without a threat to drive our economy, will we go the way of Middle Kingdom Egypt, of Greece, of Rome, of the British Empire? Are we capable of adapting to so great a change?

The Third World might provide the enemies the United States may be forced to seek. Or perhaps it will be Japan, the Pacific Basin, or the Germanic European Community. History suggests that we must find a threat, manufacture one, or wither as a nation for lack of one. Perhaps we can break the pattern, but few of us think we really will.

Jim Morris:

It has not been lost on the military that in our history we have had only one war without censorship of any kind, and we have lost only one. The major effect of the press is to decrease enemy civilian casualties and increase U.S. military casualties. The fire that kills civilians is, after all, suppressive fire, the purpose of which is to save GI lives. Nobody wants to kill civilians, and American soldiers know this, and are willing to accept risks to avoid civilian casualties, but somehow the press has missed this vital point. They seem to think artillery is simply a subsidy to the arms industry.

Brig. Gen. James Teal, Jr.

The press does have an effect on the military and the public's impressions of their military. Thomas Jefferson said if he were forced to choose between government and newspapers, he'd pick the newspapers. As pointed out by General Powell, the choice had nothing to do with trust. The press is an effective means of ensuring the government's accountability to the people. To do this it must be an aggressive, free, challenging, untrusting press, one that goes about its business afflicting the comfortable and championing the oppressed, and taking it out on the government.

There are other ways the press affects the military. During World War II and Korea, censorship was imposed and the American public was not privy to the instantaneous, minute-by-minute reporting they learned to expect during the conflict with Iraq. Vietnam probably brought about the changes in the way the press will be treated by military commanders in future conflicts. There were probably six hundred reporters in Vietnam during Tet. Most of them did a respectable job, while a few were obviously there to promote their own antiwar sentiments. In other instances, irresponsible behavior and reporting resulted in lines being drawn, and several reporters were eventually asked to leave Vietnam. To my mind, their conduct clearly warranted it.

During Desert Storm there were sixteen hundred news personnel in Saudi Arabia. Naturally they were all interested in frontline action, and the battle group commanders could not accommodate such a large number. An agreement was reached where a limited number were permitted to accompany the attacking forces, and their reports and videos were provided to the nonparticipants. Had the U.S. forces been stressed, the commanders may not have had time to give the news media the support they wanted or received. Even under these ideal conditions, there were several instances where I felt the press or news representatives overstepped their boundaries and caused problems, such as when the thirty-five reporters crossed into Iraq after the cease-fire and ended up in Baghdad as prisoners. Their actions could have caused the delay of U.S. troops returning home or a renewal of the fighting. A most irresponsible behavior.

American taxpaying citizens certainly have a right to know what is happening with their military, but it must be handled in a responsible manner. There were several new wrinkles in the news media's coverage of Desert Storm. Having U.S. reporters cover both sides of the conflict exposes the U.S. citizens to things that might be left unpublished or propaganda that might sway national will or cause indecisiveness by their leaders. It also provided Iraq with near real-time battlefield information and verification.

Another issue in Desert Storm was the reporters representing other countries of the coalition. Some of the countries participating with the United States did not have unified support at home. Arab citizens at home may become more anti-American when they see fellow Arabs being humiliated or suffering at the hands of Westerners.

The press is a part of the future battlefield. The commanders must plan how they will be handled. The choice is not up to the commanders as to whether they take the press along; therefore, they should plan to use the press to their advantage. The commanders must still do everything necessary to control the battlefield. Cellular phones and satellite communications provide a means for the reporter to give real-time coverage on what is taking place. If this provides valuable information to the opposing force commanders, then it must not be allowed.

Brig. Gen. George J. Walker

As proven during Desert Shield/Storm, the media has learned to make good use of analysts to speculate on military operations. Most of the analysts are former military persons. Analysts are educated and trained in the same military system as those who plan military operations. Given the same set of circumstances affected by the enemy, weather, and terrain, the media analysts and war planners will reach the same or at least similar conclusions. This may mean that in future military operations the media will have to be asked to suppress their analysts so as not to reveal future military operations. At least one such event occurred during the Desert Storm conflict. In order to guarantee operations security, the press and the military may have to become partners. Instantaneous electronic reporting by the media tends, or if CNN reports something, ensures that it is immediately known by both sides in a conflict.

Bob Wall:

The Gulf War victors could not have won in Vietnam. They could not have won because they were a conventional force and Vietnam was not a conventional war. Vietnam was a terrorist war. We lost because our forces were not structured to fight terrorists. If we had made it conventional by invading North Vietnam, as in Korea, that would have brought in the Chinese. You may remember we called Korea a "police action," which it surely was not. Vietnam should have been recognized as a police action too, which would have set the proper perspective. The conclusion to be drawn from this hypothesis is that our defense forces will not be fully prepared for the future until a substantial portion of them is structured to win a war like Vietnam.

The South Vietnamese people were terrorized into supporting the Viet Cong because the joint U.S.-Vietnamese military did not deny the Viet Cong access to them. Our forces were not, and are not, designed to uphold the law against terrorism. Protection of civilians from terrorism is a police job, and soldiers are not effective as police. Soldiers are trained to kill. Police are trained to enforce the rule of law. To add to the problem, the media essentially overlooked the terrorism in Vietnam. For example, in Quang Nahi Province in I Corps in 1966 there was a succession of uncooperative village chiefs who were "disemboweled" by the VC in the middle of the night by torchlight in front of their families, or vice versa, which never made the press. That piece of terrain was vital to the VC. The only way they could actually control it was through terrorism, so that is what they used.

The point here is that the U.S. and Vietnamese military were given the job of defeating the VC, but they had no counter-terror capability. They failed to understand VC strategy. That was a leadership mistake. Contact with the enemy was only made when VC and NVA forces wanted it (ambushes), so we usually lost. Our military were doing the best they could, but the Kremlin had done their homework (collected the essential intelligence on U.S. forces) and selected terrorist strategy, along with its cover name "Wars of National Liberation," as the way to best the West. Our failure to pick a better counter-strategy was inexcusable, because the prototype was readily available. The British, when confronted with a similar problem in Malaysia, accurately named the enemy "Communist Terror-ists," and called the war an "Emergency." Then they devel-oped a rural police force and intelligence system to both cope with the terrorists and protect the people, so support was denied to the terrorists. The British gave their police primary responsibility and used their military as support for the police against military formations.

An attempt was made to develop a counterterrorist force and intelligence system in Vietnam in the form of the Phoenix program, but it came very late and was not fully supported. The military was determined to win the war on their terms, and the CIA accurately predicted that the media would jump on Phoe-nix as an assassination program, and the military sought to get rid of it at the first opportunity. The Vietnamese and CORDs [Civil Operations and Revolutionary Development] were given responsibility for Phoenix, and without professional intelligence personnel, it began to be abused. Then CORDs Chief Robert Komer added the body count feature, which included reward money, and the program got out of hand. (An accurate account of Phoenix capability and potential can be found in the book *The Advisor* by Cpt. John Cook, the Phoenix advisor for two years in Di An District, Bien Hoa Province, III Corps.)

What the United States did not have at the time of Vietnam, and still does not have, is a leadership core that is fully educated in both conventional and unconventional warfare and has both the integrity and authority to call the shots in the best interest of our country. This is primarily a National Security Council job, but it also requires a president who "changes generals until he gets a winner" and Congressional armed forces and intelligence committees that are learned and put country ahead of all political considerations.

Our leaders, and the media, are particularly uneducated and unsophisticated when it comes to "unconventional action." They have been stuck on the term "covert action" for forty years or more. When the Agency undertakes unconventional action it is automatically reported by the media as covert action because it is being done by the Agency, and then everybody says the Agency is not professional because it failed to keep its action covert. The point here is that we have to be capable of a whole span of action and counteraction between conventional military action and covert action. Otherwise we will not be prepared to deal with the future.

The Provincial Reconnaissance Units [PRUs] were the epitome of unconventional action in Vietnam. They beat the VC at their own game. They had a far better body count percentage than any other force in the country. They started out as counterterrorists with the objective of stopping the VC terrorist program. They eventually attracted attention by decapitating a few VC in one province as a warning to others, but the media identified the counterterrorists as an Agency program, and said that really all is *not* fair in love and war, so the Agency began its withdrawal. Its overt move was to change the counterterrorists' mission to reconnaissance and their name to PRUs, but the media had smelled blood and would be satisfied with nothing less than a kill.

The PRUs consisted of a platoon of tough guys in each province (men whose families had been terrorized, mercenaries, and former VC) who were targeted on the VC infrastructure. They knew the territory, spoke the language, had friends in the target areas, and were prepared to pay the price. These indigenous fighters, with Agency training and support, were, in most every province, the most effective unit on our side. They became the backbone of Phoenix, and then they were disowned by the Agency. They represented the essence of the concept that should be used in "low-intensity conflicts" to win and avoid committing conventional American forces in an unfamiliar role: that is, to have a component of the U.S. defense mechanism be responsible for training native-born to do the job and leadership that can accurately define their function for the host government and the U.S. public.

Of course, indigenous rural swat teams cannot do the whole job by themselves. As terrorist units are negated it becomes necessary to have regular police who can take control of the freed territory and return life to normal under local law and civil administration. Without the support of the people, the VC and NVA military units could not have remained in the area. Their lines of supply were too long to survive without the aid of the local people, so they would be forced to fight or withdraw. The irony is that American casualties would have been reduced to a minimum, and the Vietnamese would have had the pride of

133

doing the job themselves. This is not oversimplification. It is merely identifying the fact that conventional military should not have been asked to do this job. Then, when they failed to make adjustments in their strategy, they should have been taken to task.

What we need is a component in the U.S. defense forces that focuses on terrorism and insurgency in the Third World as police work and develops a training cadre that can go anywhere and train native-born to be police, both rural SWAT teams and regulars. This means a greater than ever focus on language training and a whole new focus on personnel qualifications. It means a major adjustment by the military in their perspective on how to win in the Third World. It means much greater emphasis on intelligence than has ever been the case in our history. It means education of our people as how to wage war against terrorists. It means someone is going to have to attain éminence grise status so he or she can label ambitious but unqualified congressmen and senators for what they are. And the leadership of the Vietnam War is going to have to eat more crow in the history books.

The fact that we once had a component of USAID that dealt with police training, and that they were in Vietnam, has not been overlooked. Their personnel were more military than anything else and they had a hard time surviving because they were second-class citizens to the military. Their U.S. advisors were ex-urban cops who had no experience with terrorism or intelligence, let alone jungle warfare, so their contribution was minimal. Because of this, and the general antipathy to Third World conflicts after Vietnam, their mission and organization were abandoned by the Congress. No effort was made to review why they had failed; they were simply written off the books. So in Nicaragua, Angola, Afghanistan, and Cambodia,

Communism continued to terrorize populations, and we stood by not having learned how to help.

In terms of how to go about reorganizing for future Third World insurgency and terrorism, the first step is to recognize bureaucracy as the main enemy. The Congress, the military, the media, and the people are all career oriented in their present environment, and fear the unknown. This is the core of the problem! Rather than simply identifying the problem and not provide an answer, the following is suggested:

We must have a truly rational and inspirational leadership, willing to make changes, which is pretty hard to come by. At the moment, the best-equipped person in our country to take on such a job would appear to be General Norman Schwartzkopf. Consider that he looked at the problem in the Gulf, came up with a strategy that fitted that particular situation, and, despite a lack of experience in the desert, pulled off one of the greatest military successes in history. He had been in Vietnam and admittedly disapproved of the "strategy" tried there. Certainly he has the professionalism, reputation, flexibility, and personality to pull it off. He has the ability to educate most of the official parties involved and thwart their bureaucracies. Certainly he would benefit current efforts to limit spending and a whole lot of our mothers, fathers, and loved ones would breath a giant sigh of relief.

Actually, this is a unique opportunity in our history to make such a major adjustment. The country has been buoyed up by the victory in the Gulf and has a proven hero who is not obligated to anyone. As an expert in military matters he can jump right into the problem and bring along a whole flock of bureaucrats who would otherwise resist change until their retirement, by which time a whole new succession of bureaucrats would be in place. His ability to deal with the media would be a huge asset, and certainly the people would trust him. It might be tough to convince him to take the job because of the "quit when you are ahead" syndrome, but the challenge would probably be irresistible. In the interests of future generations of servicemen, and their families, the powers that be are urged to bite this bullet. Please consider that to have lost in Vietnam is bad enough, but not to have learned doubles the tragedy.

Dr. Ray Cline

If the intelligence system is flexible and realistic and reliable, pluralism will survive. It cannot survive if we don't know what's going on around the rest of the world.

Today it's a different world, and we've got to focus on many countries and disputes, Arab-Israeli, India-Pakistan, African and Latin American problems. With so many problems, and we had better study them all, and I think we need more intelligence rather than less.

Human beings are not very knowledgeable about international affairs. They are interested in their own affairs. We have to have an elitist intellectual system—an intelligence system that will tell policy makers what to do. That's important, but let's put as much public information out in the media and in the public domain and in Congress and everywhere as we can. Let's declassify as much as we can, because then people will understand a little better.

But I'm afraid that most human beings form their central ideas when they're about twenty-five years old, and they don't change very much. It's only the intellectuals and the academics who, although they are often wrong, can change their views. I think what we've got to do is make more of what I call "strategic intelligence" but including the information available to the people of the world. We also have to focus on strategic analysis of international affairs so we can tell the government what to do. That is the job of the CIA.

Jim Morris:

We didn't seem to have micro-management in the Gulf. There was too much of it in Vietnam, and certainly too much at Desert One in the Iran raid. If any civilian authority again considers jumping the chain of command downward I would suggest the following experiment: Send your watch out for repair. Then send four or five guys down to shoot at the watchmaker. Then send another four or five guys down to shoot back to protect the watchmaker. Then insist on coaching him through the watchmaking process over the telephone. Then see if the goddamn watch runs.

Why did the United States and U.S.S.R. fare badly in Vietnam and Afghanistan? When LeMay threatened to bomb them back to the Stone Age, he didn't realize they were already back in the Stone Age. In both cases the other side had no way to quit, and we did.

When you're far enough ahead of the second-place guys you can decline quite a lot and still be ahead. History tells us, though, that we will probably let preparedness slide until we are no longer number one, and then have to play catch-up. It should be remembered that, after we have both dismembered our nuclear arsenals, the Soviets will still have over half the tanks in the world.

Col. Michael Hayden

FRIENDS IN UNEXPECTED PLACES

With the last Yugoslav checkpoint behind us, the train slipped through the pass at Slivnitsa and gathered speed as it entered Bulgaria and descended toward Sofia and the Thracian plain. The ground all around was dry, the vegetation sparse. The unseasonable and unexpected barrenness did little to help my mood. I had just entered, with my family, one of the most Communist of Communist countries—a country implicated in the shooting of the Pope, one that had killed a dissident in London in broad daylight with a poisoned umbrella tip, a state sometimes called the sixteenth republic of the Soviet Union. I was to be air attaché, and my mission would be to observe and report on the armed forces of one of the most secretive societies on the planet.

An older gentleman engaged me in conversation in the passageway of the car. I was happy to practice my Bulgarian but had to assume he was DS (Durzhavna Sigurnost, state security, a little brother of the KGB), and so my words were guarded. Speaking freely is the first attribute of democracy to atrophy in a closed society. In our house for the next two years, my wife and I would pass important thoughts to each other or to the children by writing on a child's sketch pad, the kind that erases when you lift the plastic page. It was months after we returned to the States before we felt comfortable talking about our schedules over the telephone.

In Bulgaria, I was prepared to disdain Communism. I was prepared to feel kinship with my fellow Americans and my NATO colleagues. I was even prepared to respect and appreciate the Bulgarian people; learning anothers language offers a unique window into their soul.

But I was not prepared to develop deep and lasting friend-
ships with the military attachés of the Warsaw Pact. We came
from different cultures and different political systems; none of
us could speak the other's language. But to this day I think of
these men often, worry over their welfare, and consider
them—if you pardon the expression—my comrades. The
bonds of profession, of shared experience, drew me closer to
them than I ever expected. They were very different individually, but there was something that drew them, and me, together. Let me share a few examples.

THE COLONEL

The Colonel arrived only a few weeks before us, replacing the
Polish general who had been doyen of the attaché corps. The
Colonel's thinning hair was gray and closely cropped; his face
was permanently ruddy, and his neck always seemed ready to
burst the collar of his uniform shirt. He was a generation older
than I. As a young man, he had been a tanker in the Red Army
during the Great Patriotic War. He reminded me of my grandfather, and he rarely failed to note the difference in our ages.
His speech was surprisingly laced with references to the deity
and he rarely commented on the future without reminding his
listener, "If it is God's will."

Within weeks of his arrival, the Colonel hosted the entire
attaché corps, to celebrate Polish Army Day. He spoke from a
prepared text, extolling the virtues of socialism and cataloguing
the offenses of the West, NATO, and the United States. I
didn't know the Colonel well at this time and I thought his
words uncommonly harsh, so I was a little surprised when he
sought me out during the reception that followed. He was
solicitous, making sure I had the drink and food I wanted. As I

left he gripped my hand in both of his and thanked me for coming. His speech was the last criticism of the West I ever heard him utter.

We became friends and would share impressions about children, life, politics, peace, and war. Once he asked me to visit his embassy to give my personal impression of a visit General Jaruzelski had just completed in the United States. I armed myself by reading *Time*, the USIA wireless file, and transcripts from State Department press briefings and went to his embassy. A young receptionist ushered me into a marble-walled reception room and offered me cola, mineral water, and coffee. The Colonel entered, sat down, and asked his questions. He took occasional notes and then asked more penetrating questions about American life and politics. When he was through I had created a debt, and I collected by asking for his personal observations of the Bulgarian military leadership. He had considerably more access than any NATO attaché and I found his answers at least as candid as my own.

As I was preparing to leave I decided to ask one more unrelated question—to go, insofar as it is possible for an attaché, to what a reporter would call "off the record." Several years earlier as the intelligence officer at a tactical fighter wing, I had predicted that in the event of a Soviet invasion (which seemed likely), the Polish army would resist and fight as organized units at the regimental and perhaps even at the divisional level. Did he agree? There was a long pause, then a deep sigh. Finally, he simply said, "It would have been a catastrophe."

THE GENERAL

One bright afternoon, I was sitting in the great hall of the Czech embassy viewing a film on the Red Army's triumphal march through Slovakia and on to Prague. Since a Czech brigade had been attached, the events had been absorbed by the Czech armed forces as their own cause for celebration. But mostly the talk was of the Red Army, the "undefeatable" Red Army, the adjective permanently attached to the title the way "crack" would later be affixed to Saddam's Republican Guards.

The speaker was a Czech general, an older man, sincere and sensitive, whose shyness was made more endearing by his crossed eyes. He struggled in Bulgarian, which his native Czech and adopted Russian seemed to fracture irredeemably. Again and again, the undefeatable Red Army and the undying gratitude of his people for liberation. One could not live in the East and not feel the effect of the Second World War in a way we in the West no longer experience. It is more real, more immediate. Even those who might believe that the Soviet Army was now an occupying force seemed to recognize that it was an occupation that had been bought in blood. "*Eto fakt*," I would be told. "It is a fact."

But this day I had a few facts of my own, such as Western Czechoslovakia hadn't been liberated by the Red Army. My dad had done it, or more correctly, a lot of his friends in the U.S. Army had. As toasts were being offered left and right, I resisted the temptation to salute my dad and his friends, but I did approach the General later in the evening. "*Eto fakt*," he responded to my short history lesson.

A few weeks later the General approached me privately. Could I get him some texts of the war on the Western Front written by Westerners, but in Czech or even Russian? I tried, checking USIA and asking my Washington contacts to look in local bookstores. I had my family in Pittsburgh check the university, a school with a library well known for its interest in

Eastern Europe. Nothing. Xenophobia isn't confined to the East.

Later, under President Havel, the people of Czechslovakia could celebrate the liberation freely. The attaché who reported tens of thousands of Czechs gathered around once forlorn, lonely, and untended markers and monuments constituted some of the most emotional reportage to come from the region, in an era when emotional reportage was commonplace.

For Christmas I sent the General and his wife a bottle of California wine, an LP of the Glenn Miller orchestra, and a book on the Second World War. It was a coffee table book, good for its type, with appropriately condensed text, good photos, and excellent maps. It was my best shot.

The General later thanked me, not a pro forma, diplomatic thank you, but one volunteered heartily. I said I was sorry for the English text. No, he replied, the maps and photos tell the story. "And the music"—his hands and hips began to sway—"thank you for the music." I still picture him in his flat—pouring over a map of the Ardennes, winter 1944, with the strains of "In the Mood" filling the room.

The General made a short address at my good-bye party. Still speaking in almost unintelligible Bulgarian, he almost casually referred to United States as *"velika"* an adjective that characterized the United States as great, in the same way that Frederick or Catherine were great, or Easter was a great day (*velik den*) of the church year. In a last, private conversation, I remarked on his choice of words. *"Eto fakt,"* he responded, smiling, eyes crossed.

THE BURGERMEISTER AND THE ALTAR BOY

East German attachés always seemed different. Maybe it was the decades-long diet of West German television or perhaps the not-so-banked fires of national identity. Whatever it was, they seemed freer, more candid, less constrained than their Pact allies.

And so I was disappointed when Germann—the good-living, portly, free with his advice (don't eat too much, don't drink too much) representative of the East German Army—joined his Eastern European comrades in not attending a reception at my apartment for a visiting U.S. Army colonel. The colonel was the right-hand man of the political advisor to the commander of all U.S. forces in Europe, a fact I had assumed would be an attraction rather than a repellant. The day after my boycotted reception, Germann approached me at a lunchtime social, apologized for his absence, and claimed that he had been on business in Varna, a seaside town hundreds of kilometers from the capital.

"Bullshit," I told him. "None of you guys came." No, no he insisted. He really wanted to meet my guest. I decided to put Germann to the test. We were taking our guest to a local restaurant that night, and if he really wanted to meet him, he could just show up there. "What time?" he asked, adding, "Make sure you sit in back."

It was a neighborhood place, dark, smoky, with a musty smell that made you think of life in Europe a half-century or more ago. We arrived a little after seven and walked over the unswept wooden floors toward the rear. There was Germann, in the shadows and cigarette smoke, practically filling a booth by himself. "*Guten Abend,* Herr Colonel," he began.

Germann was scheduled to leave a few months later. His replacement was just as warm, just as open. Except where Germann seemed to call to mind a high-living, worldly burger-meister, the new man was lean, handsome—a fitting representative of the Prussian warrior class that formed the backbone of the East German army. But he wasn't Prussian, he was Bavarian, and his family had ended up in the Soviet zone only because his father had gone there looking for work shortly after the war. It was only the first of several surprises that the new man had in store for me.

The following December, he and I and our wives had been invited to dinner at the house of the Greek military attaché. Several others—Soviets, Yugoslavs, Bulgarians—would also be there. My wife and I were going to be late. It was a holy day for Catholics and we had to attend Mass before coming to dinner. We had told our hosts, and they were accommodating, but when we arrived we felt obliged to explain briefly to the other guests why we had caused the dinner to be delayed. "Shh, yes," the German added knowingly. "It's a feast of Mary, isn't it?" My head snapped in his direction. "Yes, the Immaculate Conception."

"Ja, ja."

We continued the conversation as we sat down to dinner, and the German began to recite the opening prayers of the Mass in Latin. "*Et introibo ad altare Dei.*" I will go to the altar of God. "The God who gives joy to my youth," I responded. It was a full minute of such prayer and response before we realized that we were the only ones speaking and all eyes, especially the Marxist ones, were on us. The German quickly explained that he had been an altar boy until age twelve and talk of religion soon subsided. But a bond was formed that night, the kind shaped by memories of two boys rising before dawn, fighting the winter chill and foregoing breakfast, to serve early Mass.

Every week I sent my fellow server a mint copy of *Newsweek*, so his wife could "practice her English." In April he called me from his embassy and asked if I could visit him. The United States had just bombed Libya and he wanted to know more about it. I offered to come immediately, but he suggested later in the day, in his flat where it would be more private.

I did some quick homework—once again press briefings, USIA, and the like—and set out. His wife showed us to the balcony, served us beer, and left. He didn't try to hide his agenda. Berlin wanted to know about the air raids. What could I tell him? What I had were the facts as reported publicly in the West. I gave him the narrative, but it soon became clear that what he really needed to know was whose version of events was true. The Americans had one story, the Libyans another. The Eastern European press was replaying the Libyan accounts (without comment) and I suspected their intelligence services knew little more. I cautiously embellished the narrative with what I knew of standard operations, each point reinforcing the American version of events. "But what of losses?" he asked. "One F-111, no more." "And Lybian claims?"—a not unreasonable question from a country defended by the same systems that Libya had had at its disposal.

"My friend," I responded, "feel free to doubt our claims of bomb damage; it will be more than the Libyans admit but could be less than our pilots first reported. But believe our numbers on lost aircraft. Every news organization in America now knows the units involved and aggressive reporters are already camping out at or near our bases. We cannot hide losses from the families of our men. They will learn and they will tell the press and everyone will know. Believe our numbers." He nodded and made a note. End of lecture: Free Press 101.

Over a second beer my friend volunteered information on a visit his defense minister had recently made to Bulgaria. He had arranged the visit and he was now paying me back for my candor. I put on a grateful face, but this time I thought that giving had been far better than receiving.

In the mid-1980s a Western attaché in a Warsaw Pact country lived an exciting life. He was essentially an adult delinquent, his diplomatic passport affording him protection against consequences of minor transgressions—as long as he didn't present an armed, eighteen-year-old conscript guarding an installation miles from the capital with problems too tough to handle.

Like a Plains Indian, we were proud to be "taking coup," touching the enemy but not hurting him. And "taking coup" was running a Volvo 760GLE the length of a Warsaw Pact convoy—Diet Coke and Doritos on the front seat, Willie Nelson on the car stereo—recording vehicle types, registration numbers, and unit identifiers.

Over time, however, the excitement has waned and the place names and orders of battle that were once so important have faded from memory. Now, only the people remain, their image crisp and clean against a backdrop of a history that none of us could have imagined.

Editors' comment:

Mike Hayden tells of venturing into a critical and strategic arena that is changing too fast for the world's bureaucratic processes to manage—the former Soviet Bloc. Mike's piece took a long time getting through the clearance process. Like many others, he must choose his topics carefully when he writes for an unclassified publication. Yet he found a way to focus on one of our most crucial security issues, the changes in Eastern Europe and the former U.S.S.R.

When we asked him for this piece, he was still a Director of Defense Policy at the National Security Council. While he was there, part of his job was writing speeches for Brent Scowcroft, the National Security Advisor. Today, Mike has moved on to become Chief of the Air Force Secretary's Group. He's one of the bright lights inside the system. There's no telling where he'll end up next.

We hope he'll get back into Eastern Europe and the former USSR. Many of the decisions that will shape the future of the United States and the world are now being made by today's bureaucrats, based on slim familiarity with the drastically changed situation in these emerging democracies. We must realize that the nations we historically feared and distrusted are made up of people whose national fates, like are own, are decided by a few dozen cabinet-level officials. In times such as these, we cannot afford to make the wrong decision.

The Future

1. What do you see as the single greatest threat to security in the coming decade? In the coming century?

2. If you had to guess at the map of world powers in ten years, where would the flash points be? in twenty years?

3. Many analysts believe that low-intensity conflict, counterterrorism, counterinsurgency, and counter-narcotics will be the threats we must combat in the coming century. If you agree, how would you suggest we improve our performance in these areas? If you disagree, say what threats you see as most compelling.

4. We are entering a period of massive reduction in force and restructuring of the world's armed forces. If you could advise the world's policy makers, how would you guide this process to maintain and improve readiness and strike capability while reducing the size of today's forces?

5. What improvements would you like to make in the way force is projected on the conventional battlefield? on the unconventional battlefield?

6. What have we learned about low-intensity and regional conflict while fighting in the Third World that should change the way we approach such combat in the future?

7. What do you believe the warrior of the future will face as the greatest threat to personal survival?

8. The warrior of the future will be a techno-commando, complete with magic black boxes and satellite uplinks at his command. Describe the warrior of the future, including the dream A-team and equipment package of your choice.

9. Do you think women will play a greater combat role in warfare in the future? In Canada, Israel, and other nations, women are assuming greater combat responsibilities. The United States is slowly—and reluctantly—testing women in the field. How would you feel—or how have you felt—when fighting with women on your team or under your command?

10. What is the role of special forces and unconventional warriors in the armies of the future? What will the armies of the future be like?

11. What is the place of quick-reaction forces in the warfare of the future?

12. What is the place of human intelligence collection in the future?

13. If you had the chance to tell the warriors of the future one thing, what would it be?

Military policy analysts, strategists, and tacticians the world over are now pondering a host of decisions both urgent and difficult in nature. Should we make the right choices now, a more peaceful world may be ours before the turn of the century. Should we make the wrong choices, we will sow the seeds of a new cycle of violence, misery, and death.

How will we know if we make the right choices, when the results of a decision are often not clear for a decade or more? How can we make sure that the United States positions itself properly in the gargantuan shuffle of global allegiances and assets now taking place around the globe? If we don't know what we want, how can we get it? If we are indecisive, will the moments of opportunity to forge a greater democratic global society pass us by? How can we trust old enemies? How can we make new friends? If we are truly the single superpower on the globe, what are our new responsibilities, and what are our constraints?

The correct answers to these questions lie in the future, but it is the nature of modern technological and bureaucratic processes that the solutions we seek to the problems of tomorrow must be begun today.

So we must choose blindly, follow our instinct, use our best and most educated guesses. If we can form a vision of the future as we would like it to be, and work assiduously as a nation and internationally toward that vision, we may be able to shape the changes ahead as we wish. If we only react, and consistently fail to act boldly, we can merely hope to defend against the worst disasters as they take form.

The future envisioned by our contributors is a future in which we are training for an environment that has not yet taken form. The exponential increase in the rate of technological change may make even these guesses conservative. Planning for such a future is difficult at best. Our technological successes in Operation Desert Storm were based on military technology programs planned in the 1970s which took two decades to execute and perfect.

This new cycle of planning and execution must be flexible, developed for a multipolar world of multiple threats, be cost-effective for a peacetime economy, and be able to maintain a force projection capability second to none but infinitely mutable. Events in the Persian Gulf suggest that such a force, to be internationally acceptable and quickly deployable, must be capable of exerting the least force necessary to win in any circumstance.

We must create a new focus for our international goals and a new methodology to achieve those goals. And we must do so before we make errors in the present that will come back to haunt us in the future.

Lt. Col. Neil L. Putz:

We are living in what is arguably the most exciting, and at the same time the most crucial, period in the history of mankind. If we could look into the middle of the next century, there are alternative worlds we might see. Given these glimpses of the future, I will propose corresponding roles for the warrior class, and threats to its survival in the future environment.

152

For years we all held our breath to see whether 1984 would approach George Orwell's apocalyptic vision. We have far to go to attain the advances of Arthur C. Clarke's *2001*. What will the geopolitical factors now at work lead us to by, say, 2050?

We can easily imagine increasing efficiency and industrial power in a unified Europe. We have seen economic miracles based upon efficient societies of the Pacific Rim, particularly in Northeast Asia. The technological advances in both those areas and here in North America set these peoples on the positive side of the technology gap.

Across this widening gap we see, when we want to, the teeming billions of souls of the Third World. They are largely malnourished, impoverished, and undereducated. The raw materials of their nations fuel the growth of our planet. Their dwindling rain forests restore oxygen to our atmosphere. Needy workers from these lands either strip resources from their air, land, and waters, or they migrate to the industrialized nations to toil and subsist.

Preserving the status quo in an ever-collapsing ecological world would be a difficult task. That is, assuming that governments wish to preserve the status quo. I cannot speculate on when the downward spiral of this planet's ecology will trigger universal recognition of an outcome so dismal that our industrialized nations, the Third World nations, or *all* nations, will reach a breaking point and take positive action.

The greatest service that this planet's future warrior class could offer would be a coherent force to establish discipline over expenditure of scarce resources, enforce adherence to thoughtful, strict pollution controls, and protect scientists engaged in the reconstruction of our heretofore shattered ecological balance. What a noble cause indeed!

Why must there be force to protect these interests? Simply to

153

protect us from ourselves, the same selves who have lazily allowed this decay to continue, unchecked, since the whispered warnings have become an outcry that increases in volume from year to year.

But what if the nations of the world are unable to agree on action to save the planet? The economic stakes are too great, the rich are too comfortable and control too many governments, and there is no advantage to any politician in defending the earth. The greatest threat to the warrior class, worldwide, is that it may become the instrument of local resource "warlords" in a sort of *Mad Max* future, stripping the planet's dwindling resources in a cruel endgame of human extinction.

And what will be the twenty-first-century threats to the United States of America? The developed nations will likely have to contend with mounting frustration from Third World states who have depleted their marketable resources. They will have little left with which to bargain. Additionally, economic competitors on our own side of the technology gap will increase the pace of the ongoing search for new sources of raw materials. Ruthless economic warfare might seem to make the warrior class obsolete. Diplomacy may prevail as we seek to resolve economic crises, but assisting the frustrated, starving masses of the human crisis will require a ready force, possibly depending upon the organizational skills of the warrior class.

What will be the demographics of American society in fifty years? Within our own borders, we are today sowing the seeds of a harvest that we may reap or squander in the twenty-first century. Through sound educational policies and programs it is hoped we are fostering development of a coherent nation, with optimal harmony from within. We must do this to better enable our nation to withstand the global upheavals (political, economic, humanitarian, and ecological) that are just beginning to manifest themselves.

There will always be a mission for the warrior class. The nature of that mission is of course dictated by its parent government. Those who commit their talents toward this end vow to abide by the directives they receive. In democratic societies, the will of the people guides the government, which in turn guides the military, which in turn attracts young people to join its ranks. I pray that the world's democratic societies continue to strengthen their will toward preserving our earth, and that members of those societies seek to join the ranks of forces committed to this most crucial mission.

Now, once again, the dark side of our possible future. Perhaps the warrior class will be employed to forage for food and other resources to support ailing, declining parent nations. This would be the most heinous of all futures, with mankind making war over the last crumbs of bread as we approach final extinction.

The opponent of the future warrior is himself. As masters of the earth, mankind must develop the self-discipline to respect and preserve this planet. There may still be numerous conventional conflicts and a minor nuclear/terrorism conflict, but we are approaching the endgame.

Whether or not you share my views, you and your descendants will not be able to ignore the truth. The dinosaurs ignored the truth unwittingly. As sentient beings, the human race will either watch its own extinction with calm detachment, or actively attempt to preserve itself by socially evolving to a higher plane of environmental concern.

Yet a third possibility is a "middle road" return to the Dark Ages. This is the ultimate result of the practice of muddling through. While it is not the most desirable outcome, it presumes that the collapse of the community of nations and human society is not accompanied by total extinction of the human species. Rather, in a few thousand years we get a second chance.

This environmental threat is so insidious. Slow deterioration is not universally recognized as life-threatening. We want the immediate gratification of seeing results, like airlift of food to famine-stricken areas of the world. Our society has been slow to recognize and reward the career field of environmental repairman. Far more careers reward waste of the environment than the careers that positively reinforce it. We must all hope to see the trend improve, so that earning a living in virtually every profession is compatible with the concept that each of us must put as much into the environment as we take from it.

Maj. David P. Kutchinski:

The warrior of the twenty-first century will be no different from the warrior of the Spartan army of ancient Greece. This warrior will have a love for learning. No matter what the subject, he will jump into it and immerse himself. He will stay abreast of all modern developments in all areas of the marketplace. He will always remember the keys to success on the battlefield, given to him by former warriors. If you were to look on his bookshelf, you would find a well-worn copy of *The Art of War*, beside his copy of *Digital Techniques*.

The warrior of the twenty-first century will be a mutation of several disciplines. No longer will he spend all his time on the range or at the dojo. He will be spending more of his time in the library or laboratory. Each suit of armor created in the Dark Ages had a vulnerable spot. The new smart weapons system have the same vulnerabilities, and he will know where to look. He realizes that knowledge is a critical weapon.

He will become a student of weapons and weapons systems. Not only how to employ them, but all aspects that make them work. He will study ballistics and chemicals as they relate to warfare. He will read the latest trade literature about new equipment. Most people in industry will not be looking at their product with the experienced eye of the warrior. The manufacturer will not be aware of martial uses for his product.

Since the contractor who creates the weapons systems now and in the future will not be a warrior, the future warrior will learn metallurgy to create his own weapons and defense systems or improve upon poor designs. For example, a self-contained combat suit debuted recently. The suit has its own air conditioning, IR sensors, and SATCOM communications. Imagine this soldier's surprise when he feels the crossbow bolt penetrate his self-sealing air-conditioned suit. A bolt fired from a little guy, dressed in camouflage, in a spider hole. The great part about these suits is that, as the soldier dies, the onboard computer will tell the dying man the azimuth and velocity of the bolt that killed him—which I'm sure will be comforting.

The future warrior will be a perpetual student of the electromagnetic spectrum. The soldiers he will face in the next century will have no understanding of it. With his knowledge he will defeat the soldiers with their own systems. As soldiers rely more and more on the computer, any disruption of the links will cause confusion. Access to this link can provide the warrior with information about the kinks in the soldier's armor. The warrior will have an understanding of modern smart weapons targeting methods. With this knowledge he will defeat these weapons by knowing when he can thwart the system and when he must quell the operator. Many of the modern systems can be defeated rather cheaply by simply knowing what it expects to see.

The warrior of the twenty-first century will be unusual, to say the least. His adversaries will come in three flavors. First will be the superpower soldier. This will be the soldier who will have all the high-priced, high-tech weapons systems. He will be fat, dumb, and content believing that he is safe behind his Techno (rhymes with Maginot) line. The advertised claims of the contractors will lull him into a false sense of reality. The reality is that these new toys will only perform optimally when oper-ated and maintained by the contractor, in an environment selected by the contractor. This superpower soldier will have more of the creature comforts than any soldier in history. This is assuming that his logistics train directly behind him.

He will be led by an officer corps that is "politically correct." The ability of the officer corps to lead troops in combat will not be much of a factor anymore. With the meager budgets of the coming years the officer corps will consist of whatever makes the bean counters happy. The officer corps will have to stay politically more active than ever before to survive in their abbreviated form. This new officer corps will best be described as "Yuppies in Uniform." As the bean counters replace flesh and blood with technology the officer corps will become more concerned with career than mission. This will be an environ-ment a warrior can barely tolerate. Students of history will probably recognize this situation.

Second will be the Third World mini-powers. These soldiers will have the best modern equipment that their well-financed government can afford. They will have only superficial training on the systems with no sociological background to understand the modern technology. Their motivation will be minimal. Their leaders will have little restraint in the employment of their new toys. These tyrants will waste dreadful amounts of manpower to prove a point. As has been in the past, it will be in the future—life has little meaning to these people. The more citizens who die in a conflict the fewer the leader will have to feed or control when it is over.

The last adversary will be the non-territorial soldier. Today he is called a "terrorist," or "narco-terrorist." Motivation and signature will be the critical area where this soldier differs from the previous two. In the arena of narcotics, the take from the United States alone is about forty-one billion dollars a year. That much money can equip both groups. This soldier will be employing more and deadlier modern weapons systems to accomplish his goals at the time and place of his choosing. Whether the goal be political or narcotics motivated, this soldier will continue to grow in sophistication and effectiveness.

As the twenty-first century warrior goes into combat, he will take with him the equivalent of the modern Cray computer. With this he will crack the armor of the enemy's electromagnetic dependent weapons and C4I systems. Through his computer system he will feed the enemy's systems the intelligence they expect to see. The less sophisticated the operator, the easier it will be. Thanks to publications like *Jane's* and *Aviation Week & Space Technology*, the warrior will always have recent information. These publications will give him information on who is buying what C4I systems, and how they work. He will adapt his weapons for the situation. However, his personal sidearm will remain the Colt .45.

Once the first two types of soldiers commit to one form of action their ability to change quickly is nonexistent. When the enemy has committed to one action the warrior will strike at key targets with terrifying effectiveness. His surgical destruction will be calculated to inflict the greatest trauma to his enemy. He will disable billion dollar systems with a thousand dollar piece of gear. He will cause the enemy's smart weapons, costing millions, to blow up mock-ups, costing hundreds. Any arrogance on the part of the enemy commanders will be met with a loud and destructive death. He will be merciless. When he leaves, he will leave in his wake destruction on a scale that these armies had never dreamed.

The only enemy that the warrior will have trouble with will be the third type of soldier. The trouble will come from political restraints more than the abilities of the adversary. A paid soldier who has nothing but poverty or a refugee camp to return to will be a well-motivated adversary. The commitment of the employer of the warrior will become the key to success. Since this enemy has no territorial boundaries, the warrior must be able to operate under these same restraints. The warrior will not be effective operating under the restraints imposed by the country's State Department. Recently, the State Department has been responsible for more warrior deaths than any war. I'm sure that this will continue. Funny, how governments fear warriors, even in their own ranks.

To defeat the third type of soldier we cannot use any of the old rules or tactics. He requires a whole new textbook, the kind that was written when the warriors were the politicians.

The modern armies have forgotten that the most effective smart weapon, is a well-trained warrior.

Major Michael C. Redmond

The combat soldier of today and of the future is a new entity. Today's soldier is a composite of all races, creeds, ages, and sexes. Training, developing, encouraging, and motivating are basic tools that should be used to ensure a level of equality. A strong basis for future development is a training philosophy based on the society that produces the soldiers. This philosophy should be communicated in all training.

Modern training must be based on the emotional and psychological needs of the soldier in order to develop well-rounded, secure, and caring individuals. The Army Reserves Instructor Training Course, for example, is designed to meet this task, treating the internal chemistry of the soldier with equal importance as the external aspect.

In the past, military training attempted to mold fighting machines that reacted by instinct instead of by logic and situations. A strong training program, with a foundation psychology and sociology, helps a leader develop into a teacher who will continue to develop subordinates throughout his or her career.

Throughout time great philosophers have fed theories into society, and by doing this, also into the military. Rousseau and John Dewey developed strategies for education and training that are still applicable today. Ethics and values within an organizational structure, including the military, were developed through the teachings of Plato and Aristotle. Modern theorists Blake and Mouton devised a managerial grid for leaders to use as a self-assessment tool; Dennis Waitly's "Psychology of Winning" approach is intended to develop a confident and committed leader; Lakim teaches time management techniques for leaders.

The military must encompass the teachings of these and others into its training. A soldier must be groomed as a future leader, and to continue to grow independently, able not only to interpret, but to develop strategies and courses of action within society's vision.

Rank or position of a soldier does not automatically confer

leadership. One must be a leader, know how to lead effectively, and do whatever is necessary. Being a leader is a result of a developmental process that starts in childhood and continues through all the stages of a military career. To become a leader, a soldier must develop a personality that contains four attributes: decisiveness, support, organizational ability, and influence.

Decisiveness is key and helps to provide purpose and direction. Quick, consistent decisions based on tactical and technical facts and theoretical teachings will be required in today's new fighting strategies.

Support for one's subordinates builds morale and loyalty, which are crucial to preparation for battle.

Organizational ability is necessary in order to avoid mistakes and ensure optimum integration and performance of the unit. Delegation and coordination are important aspects of organizational ability.

The more senior a soldier, the more critical are skills as an "influencer" in command, control, and communications.

Military leadership requires that a soldier be result-oriented rather than process-oriented. Herzberg's and Maslow's theories of motivation are a good base of knowledge and training for soldiers, who must develop both themselves and subordinates. Motivation and direction are essential in a soldier's training. A malaise effect may be seen in soldiers who feel their emotional and psychological needs are not being met.

A soldier must both mirror society and be an element in society. Modern society stresses that an individual must have a vision that addresses organization, challenge, process, ethics, and skills. A soldier must have perspectives relating to society's history and concerns for the future. A soldier must exemplify society's attributes of purpose, direction, and motivation.

A soldier must be trained in professional conceptual skills, technical and tactical competency, and the communications skills necessary to do well at all levels. This allows the soldier to develop a well-defined purpose and strong sense of direction. The soldier will be adaptive, cohesive, and resilient—ready for the military of tomorrow.

Jim Morris:

Women will play a greater combat role in warfare, but I think the experiment will fail. Not that women aren't intelligent or courageous. We have to start with the plain fact that war is insanity, and I don't think many women are insane in that particular way. It's as though back at the dawn of time all the guys in the world got together and said, "Hey, what's the dumbest thing we could possibly do?" and some other Neanderthal replied, "I know, let's choose up sides and kill each other." And so they did.

The Israeli experience is frequently cited as a precedent for women in combat, but the Israelis tried women in combat and found that, although the women did fine, the protective instincts of the men came out and they failed to do their jobs for worrying about the women. In my brief career as a correspondent I encountered the same situation. I covered the invasion of Lebanon in '82, and my wife was my photographer. When it got really hairy she was cool and professional, but I totally lost it worrying about her. Finally, when it really heated up, I flat refused to take her in. When I got to the kibbutz that was our starting point I found the Israelis had made the same decision. No female correspondents allowed into Lebanon on that day.

Cpt. Linda A. Gorsuch:

Fighting with women in your command is an issue that, perhaps, combat arms people who haven't worked with women before discuss over a beer at the club. When you're in the field, in a unit where men and women work together daily, you don't have time to worry about that. You worry about getting the job done. My unit didn't deploy during Desert Storm, but I doubt anyone would have found the time to worry about the "role of women" there either. I think the reason some men worry about women in combat is because they have spent all their time in "male only" units. They imagine that things would be different if women were there. They talk about societal values and all that. I've never seen societal values compel a man to offer to dig a woman's fighting position for her or put a new tire on her truck! I doubt a man would suddenly feel compelled in combat to pull a woman's weight for her, protect her, etc. He'd be too busy trying to take care of himself.

I think women will have to play a greater role in warfare in the future. They've proven themselves consistently in recent conflicts, as well as in earlier ones. Warfighting is becoming increasingly technical, requiring skills at which women often do better than men. As an example, women tend to be more agile, with quicker reflexes than men. However, our Army will not reach its full potential until we fill all specialties by ability criteria, rather than gender criteria. If a specialty requires strength, we should identify objective standards for strength, and make everyone in that specialty meet the standard. If 99 percent of women aren't strong enough for a certain specialty, they shouldn't be allowed to hold it. But the one percent who are strong enough should not be prevented from holding it. At the same time, if 50 percent of the men already in the specialty can't meet the standard, they should not be allowed to retain it. We shouldn't allow any group to pressure us into lowering a necessary standard just so more women, or men, can qualify for a specialty. The bottom line is that the military will be a better place for everybody when we eliminate all quotas, both those that exclude women and those that unfairly favor women or other minorities.

Brig. Gen. James Teal, Jr.:

As a career intelligence officer, I never miss an opportunity to discuss the threat to United States security. Everything from drug interdiction, Special Operations, low-intensity conflicts, deployment of significant conventional forces, to nuclear forces, all contribute to negating threats to our national security. Since we can't design a specific military capability for each specific threat, we have to make do with a multifunctional military that can adapt, with minimal preparation, to meet a variety of requirements.

In light of the rapidly changed and changing world environment, there are obvious actions that can now take place without endangering our objectives. These include the reduction of the nuclear stockpile, a large cut in the U.S. general purpose forces, the closing of U.S. bases overseas, and the assumption of security responsibilities by those numerous countries that have received protection under the U.S. umbrella for so many years.

On the other hand, we must ensure we continue in our superpower status by maintaining a strong industrial base, supporting development of critical technologies, and maintaining a mix of rapid deployable and heavy forces to handle contingencies from drug interdiction and low-intensity conflict. We must also be ready to deploy conventional forces where a strong presence may be required for extended periods.

Since World War II we've had three involvements in three mid-intensity conflicts—Korea, Vietnam (maybe?), and Desert Storm. During the same time the U.S. armed forces have been involved at different levels in almost fifty low-intensity conflicts. These do not include the peacekeeping operations where we've provided our military support. Reviewing this from a strategic perspective in light of today's world, I see the potential for the use of U.S. forces in low-intensity conflict increasing.

I believe a potential short-term economic threat and a long-term military threat is developing with our allies, Japan and Germany. This provides the basis for the U.S. to keep the trade balance in balance and maintain a free flow of commerce and technology across our borders. With the proper—or improper—national attitude, both these countries possess an industrial base, the technology, and potential to become a military superpower almost overnight.

Major Richard Groller:

As we enter the new millennia the single greatest threat to national and global security is from competitive intelligence. With "peace" breaking out all over, the arena of warfare is moving more and more to the economic front. This front has a direct impact on the national wherewithal to execute successful warfare across the entire spectrum of lethal conflict, and its emphasis can be just as deadly.

The spectrum of conflict of economic warfare includes arms embargo and nuclear nonproliferation violations, illegal technology transfer, software piracy, economic blackmail—from computer viruses to nuclear blackmail—and the more mundane aspects of the stealing of secrets.

In the last few years, U.S. industry (and her global competitors) have taken a closer look at the intelligence gathering process as a matter of business policy. Taking a cue from the military and government agency professionals, the old term "industrial espionage" (with its attendant unsavory connotations) has been replaced by a new euphemism, "competitive intelligence" or CI.

The computer revolution has taken much of the drudgery out of the intelligence gathering process. Access to on-line data bases, including national and international governmental and military data bases covering order of battle, budget information, warfare system technical parameters, and sales/deployment figures, even daily tracking of flag rank military officers is all available (for a price) as accessible public records. Via modem, someone studying the health of a given military-industrial complex can amass incredible volumes of data, which can then be indexed and analyzed by data base managers. Advanced processing techniques can discern trends and forecast the actions of competitors, whether they are companies or countries, across the spectrum of marketing, merger, and acquisition. Even threat assessment is possible.

Intelligence, as the second-oldest profession ("Then Joshua, son of Nun, secretly sent out spies from Shittim, saying, 'Go, reconnoiter the land and Jericho'" Joshua 2:1) has a well-deserved reputation, honed to a fine edge by the military and intelligence services. Industrial efforts to develop a routing professional approach to CI have thus followed the procedures

167

of the established "intel" services already in existence. Like a general officer at the morning stand-up briefing, senior corporate management is being given its dose of synthesized "happy snaps" and daily "read file" input, which may well impact the day's business decisions. About the only real difference between the civilian and military process is that the "read file" in the military is usually classified, while the corporate executive's file may be marked "proprietary" or "eyes only" or "confidential" with no correlation to the government system of classification. Still, the data contained therein may be just as critical. Some major companies, such as Motorola and Pfizer,* have even gone so far as to enlist the aide of ex-intelligence officers from the CIA to establish and run their in-house intelligence departments. Here they often hid behind such innocuous titles as the Office of Technology Assessment or the Technological Forecasting Division or the Office of Strategic and Market Planning.

The fact that corporate America is assimilating these techniques is commendable. It's about time. Some visionary thinkers in global realpolitik realize the critical need for such capabilities. The question is, how good are our efforts when compared to organized competitive intelligence efforts of corporate Japan? How do we fair against the government-sponsored, professionally run economic intelligence gathering efforts of the KGB and Mossad? As you read this paragraph what facts are the military technology hunters of the competition gleaning by studying not only our products, but the R&D budgets, the markets, the corporate wherewithal to deliver what it advertises? Assessing the individual levels of hunger of U.S. companies, i.e., how serious they are about obtaining

*Jan Broughton, "Why Spy," *American Way,* May 1989, p. 44

168

business, what will their profit and loss statements look like, and are they likely targets for unfair competition or even takeover?

The U.S. industrial base is at risk, especially in the economic climate of "everything for a price." United States assets, property, and corporations are being annexed by foreign firms at a frightening rate, and global competitiveness is more and more becoming a critical issue of national survival. And while our industrial base is eroding, so is our academic base, the well-spring of the technological and economic prowess that is the basis of American might.

America is producing fewer and fewer science, mathematics, and engineering graduates. For the last several years, over half the Ph.D.s produced in American universities have been foreign born, often at foreign government expense. The pool of available, clearable (able to hold a security clearance) senior scientists is dwindling, and this will have a serious impact on the ability of the U.S. industrial base to continue the upward trend of innovation, classified, super-high technology in the military arena for years to come.

Defense cutbacks are forcing the pool of military niche market engineers to find new jobs in other sectors, often unsuccessfully. "Electronic immigrants" from India, Pakistan, and other countries with low standards of living, are further undercutting American engineering talent by working for extremely low pay via long distance. Competitive scores of American students when tested against their counterparts in the industrialized world have been consistently low. Literacy is decreasing, and with it the hopes and dreams of many of our youth.

What is required in order to reverse this trend is a two-fold effort by the U.S. government and U.S. industry. The first fold hinges on a *Sputnik* era revival in science and math education, with the government and industry providing the impetus and expertise. The second is a need for a strong national economic policy (one currently does not exist). The two of these together, perhaps married to a great civilian-led high-tech enterprise, like support for the Space Exploration Initiative, could lead to a virtual renaissance in science and engineering futures and secure the viability of the U.S. technological and economic base into the next century.

One lesson learned from Desert Storm is that the scene of the battleground and the scene of the proving ground will continue to become one in the same. Both inner and outer space will be areas ripe for potential conflict. Between the drive for high-technology and the quest to maximize human potential, the armed forces of the future will be lethal, capable of lightning reaction and maneuver time, and, of necessity, be semi-autonomous.

Interconnection and autonomy will be the key. Holistic concepts of defense and offense will be intertwined, based upon enhanced abilities to communicate at all echelons. What then can be forecast as the technologies of choice for the future force planner of tomorrow? As a technowarrior of today, I can see these technologies broken into three areas of extrapolation: evolutionary, revolutionary, and radical technologies.

Evolutionary technologies are direct descendants of current systems or systems currently under research and development and thus based upon conservative estimates of growth trends. We would reasonably expect to see continued research and expansion of the new high ground of space, for example, with satellite systems used to tie together a global network for navigation, reconnaissance, global positioning, targeting, communications, and a myriad of other functions. This would of necessity be augmented by an active space command, with a fleet of workhorse spacecraft to ensure sustainment and survivability, as well as an extraterrestrial base of operations, most likely the moon, a string of space stations, or a manmade satellite placed strategically in orbit at a Lagrange point (L-5 for example).

Another evolutionary trend would be in the area of self-contained body armor (Kevlar/Spectra/Gortex/Titanium mixtures) that would be lightweight and provide ballistic protection as well as protection against lasers. It could provide concealment from infrared and ultraviolet surveillance, a heads-up tactical display, integrated communications, and NBC protection. Still another area would be electronics and energy weapons, including tactical and strategic directed energy weapons, such as lasers and plasmas; electromagnetic weapons, such as microwave and radio frequency weapons, electromagnetic pulse generators and railguns; robotic and artificial intelligence/expert guided systems of all sorts; and miniaturized communications systems that are jam-proof, encrypted, all-weather capable, have a one meter or less self-location capability, and are capable of video teleconferencing.

Yet another area of evolutionary change can come in the area of nonlethal weapons technologies. With increases in police action–style conflict and the move to decrease collateral damage and eliminate the political incentive of martyrs, innovation in this area is a logical growth path. Nonlethal technologies have a multitude of tactical applications, including fouling the engines of air-breathers (viscosification agents); "dud"-ing electronics (non-nuclear electromagnetic pulse); blinding of sophisticated target-acquisition systems or dazzle human operators (hand-held lasers and isotropic radiators); and crowd dispersal (using transient effect generators or nonlethal chemical agents). Just to name a few.

171

The next area of extrapolation is revolutionary technology. Revolutionary technologies are the progeny of areas of fundamental research that is going on today. They are not yet mature and their potential is not yet realized. Examples of this could include superconductivity and its derivative, the Meissner effect, with their promises of lossless transmission of energy and the capability to create all-terrain vehicles that silently levitate above the earth's surface; power economies that could lead to Cray-equivalent supercomputers downsized to hand-held devices; genetic engineering, with its potential for biological weapons and protection from biological weapons, cloning, and the possibility of the creation of android armies tailored to specific environments; weather modification, with its impact on tactical situations as well as its potential large-scale environment, economic, and national implications; psychotronics, with its promise to maximize human potential and the powers of the mind through precognitive remote perception, telekinesis, and extrasensory perception, as well as its threat to security through mind control and psychoactive brainwave entertainment, controlled offensive behavior, and intrusive perception-/action at a distance; and computer and algorithmic advances based on the new theories of chaos, fuzzy logic, and nonlinear dynamics, with their promises of modeling systemic variables currently too unwieldy to model.

Finally, radical technologies are functions of breakthroughs, fed by systems synergism, serendipity, imagination, individual genius, and the "Eureka!" effect. Examples of this would be breakthroughs in high-energy physics that today border on the metaphysical, and could include research into the nature of reality, time travel, local and nonlocal quantum effects, virtual state engineering (direct engineering of the Schrodinger equation), controllable A-field effects to include macroscopic

172

Bohm-Aharanov effects (i.e., action at a distance with no perceptible/detectable mechanisms), as well as theories on hyperspace, multiple dimensions, and the collective unconscious.

Brig. Gen. George J. Walker

Human intelligence collection has always been important to military operations. Unfortunately national and military leaders do not always feel comfortable with HUMINT operations, primarily because they do not understand covert HUMINT operations. We witnessed the dismemberment of HUMINT capabilities during the Carter administration and as late as 1986 a particular CINC directed the cessation of associations with covert HUMINT sources in an area of the world that was then and continues to be a great concern to the United States.

Most commanders who feel uncomfortable with covert HUMINT efforts simply fail to understand that the development of meaningful covert HUMINT sources takes years and not hours. If the United States truly wants to determine the intentions of adversary leaders, that can best be accomplished by well-funded, long-term human sources.

We Americans tend to rush to judgment based on the last war fought without regard to the actual threat posed by potential adversaries. An example might be the effort to create light forces so those forces could be rapidly deployed, only to find ourselves in a Middle East war where, other than air mobile forces, light forces would not have been effective. The war in the Gulf was a war requiring the use of heavy armored forces. Our military forces should be composed of a mixture of heavy and light forces that will be able to meet all future contingencies. Our force structures are too often based on the whims of four star commanders with little or no regard for the actual threat. We need force development based on threat, not advocacy.

In the near and long term our military forces must be capable of defeating threats that include Third World adventurism, terrorism, and narcotics traffickers as well as adversary conventional heavy and light forces. I do believe the forces can be reduced, but those forces must be well equipped and smart weapons are a must.

As far as future hotspots go, while not all of these would create U.S. involvement, over the next ten years, these areas must be closely watched so as to not upset the balance of power in any given region of the world: Middle East, Korea, Libya, and regional conflicts in Eastern Europe. In twenty years we must add: Japan and Germany. Both will be in constant economic competition with the United States. We must guard against economic competition leading to a twenty-first-century-style trade war.

Dr. Ray Cline

The question of human intelligence collection is a very critical issue, but I probably have a different view from many people. Right now there is an explosion of data that it is necessary to examine, sift, assess, and create into an analytical structure that can give policy makers some advice. There is a lot of classified information, but I'd say that at least 80 percent of it is unclassified. If you don't understand the structure of foreign societies, and the American society, you don't know what to do. I always saw myself as a researcher and an analyst, even though I became deeply involved in clandestine operations and even secret covert operations—psychological and paramilitary operations. We need more clandestine operations now. Human source agent collection is crucial for us, because if you can get inside a foreign government and be sure that what the agents are telling you is the truth, then you get an insight into what they are trying to do.

However, we should have two or three times as many intelligence sources as we have had in the past, because we concentrated mainly on the Soviet Union and China and they were hard targets—very closed societies. We now have to look at many countries of the world, including the Europeans and certainly the Asians.

The key problem is not the secret source, however, but the analysis and research. Then you provide some options and potentialities for policy making. An intelligence system is not intended to make policy, but should describe probabilities and options and let the policy makers decide what they ought to do.

Although covert operations are going to be less important in the future, they will continue, largely through psychological warfare rather than paramilitary operations. Occasionally, we may have to conduct a paramilitary operation to stop some dictatorship. I would like to see us do that more thoughtfully than we have. If you cut off a dictator quickly, then the society will survive. You see what has happened after seventy years of Soviet dictatorship. It's very hard for the Russians to change their style, their manner. They want to have a relatively democratic society, particularly with their economic strength and wealth, and they don't know how to do it. And after seventy years of dictatorship, most of the leadership people don't know how to do it. So we have to recognize that we should occasionally, very occasionally, move in to change the minds and hearts of the Russians, and other peoples. If there is a military country that is damaging to our interests, we should also occasionally run a paramilitary covert operation, if it can succeed.

The world has changed so rapidly with the disintegration of the Soviet Union that our biggest problem now is how to sustain Russian democratic pluralist behavior and keep them from reverting to dictatorship. Also, and here is where psychological and covert operations might be useful, how can we persuade the Chinese to change their minds? They still believe totally in their four cardinal principles: socialism, one-party system, dictatorship, and the thoughts of Marx, Lenin, and Mao Tse Tung. Well, that's just a lot of gobbledygook. The Chinese aren't very interested in ideology. They are very power oriented, and given what Deng Xiaoping did at Tiananmen Square, we have a real challenge. The Chinese want to keep their power and keep it as a dictatorship. Many Chinese believe this is right, because they are afraid of chaos. There have been many civil wars and disasters in China for six thousand years, but we must persuade them that being a little more inclined toward a democratic pluralist process would be useful to them. That's what our psychological goal ought to be right now.

Despite the importance of the Chinese, whatever they do, and the importance of the Russians, whatever they do, there are a lot of Third World countries that are trying to kill their neighbors. In a country like Iran, for instance, there is a Shiite fundamentalist group that always fought Iraq and will probably always fight Iraq. They wanted to destroy Saudi Arabia. They haven't been able to. Religious fundamentalists are going to be a big problem for us ahead, partly because the Cold War has ended and we're not very likely to get out there and start another war to protect the Middle East. With the collapse of Russia, we're pretty much the only superpower. China is a secondary power, but I think for the next twenty years we won't have to worry too much about them, if we can get them to be a little more relaxed and democratic.

Religious and minority groups, which are very culture bound and dedicated to their own fundamentalist cultural systems, will be a problem. The Arabs and the Israelis and the Iranians are all very different and they all want to have their own way. Low-intensity conflict is going to be a very important issue—one which can get out of hand and cause us a great deal of difficulty. Counterterrorism and counternarcotics are difficult problems for us, and I would like to see improvement in our performance in that area. We probably should have a quasi-overt/covert operation, which would get a lot of public support, that would prevent any of these Third World countries from causing a civil war or raising a lot of hell and murdering hundreds of thousands of people. Somehow we have got to find some way to do it, to prevent that from happening.

Sgt. Maj. J.D. "Rowdy" Yeats:

Warriors of the future, be professional in all of your endeavors. Be the best soldier you can be. You owe it to yourself, your fellow soldiers, those soldiers under you and those soldiers that have passed before you. Don't assume anything. Your goal is to become the authority within your Military Occupation Specialty [MOS]. You want the rest of the company, battalion, brigade, or division to come to you for guidance on each and every topic associated with your MOS. You must become proficient and competent on every piece of equipment that is organic to your unit. There is nothing worse than an amateur in combat. He can make an awkward predicament become a life-endangering situation.

177

The greatest future threat to Special Operations Forces is the amount of high-technology equipment they are required to carry into the operational area to conduct the mission. There is a saying among Special Forces types—"We have two hundred pounds of lightweight equipment." The Special Forces soldier is being loaded down with mission-essential equipment and having to leave individual equipment in isolation. Worse yet, we are seeing personal survival equipment being placed in resupply packages that are to be air-dropped in at a later date. In addition, individual basic ammunition loads are being reduced to accommodate the high-tech equipment.

The warriors of the future will not be different from the warriors of past wars. The characteristic traits will be the same. However, the difference between the warriors of the future and the warriors of the past will be the battlefield. The warrior's combat instincts will still be intrinsic and his nature will be spiritual, but his knowledge of the battlefield will be based upon technological information. We know that the battlefield can become a confusing place, even the simplest of actions can become very complicated. The task for the future warrior is to find a way to assimilate this new battlefield technological information and incorporate their own combat sense to accomplish the mission.

My dream A-Team: I have a deep belief that the present configuration of Special Operations Groups should be done away with. In its present configuration, team leaders and team sergeants have little say in whom they receive on their team. Future Special Operations missions should select personnel from a pool of qualified Special Forces soldiers. This accomplishes several things. One, the competitive nature and the desire to be selected would require the individual Special Forces soldier to be the best in his business. Two, while waiting for the next mission selection, soldiers would be allowed to train in their individual MOS or develop or improve those skills in which they are lacking. Three, team leaders and team sergeants would start to have more control over those soldiers who are in the pool. If you want to be selected you damn well better know how to soldier.

My dream A-Team would consist of career soldiers/warriors who were of the rank of E-6 and higher. The team leader would be a senior Cpt. and the XO a senior 1st Lt. The average age for the team would be 28. The average Physical Fitness Test score for the team would be 300. The Military Occupation Skills [MOS's] on the team would be determined by the mission. All members of the team would be crossed-trained in three additional MOS's, and have at least a 2-2 rating in one or more languages. Team members would be required to have at least 14 years of formal education and have some type of technical skill (welding, electrician, mechanic, etc.). Team members would be required to be experts in individual soldiering skills. High ethical and moral standards would be expected of each team member.

Equipment: Team equipment would be consistent with current technology. The mission would have operational funds for "off-the-shelf" purchase of mission equipment. Specialized mission equipment requirements would be conceptualized and developed prior to the team going into isolation. The vast majority of special operation missions can be accomplished by off-the-shelf equipment.

SFC Barry Rhodes

THE FUTURE OF THE NCO

It's a cliché. The more things change the more they stay the same. This has been true about the Army since its very beginning. The NCO, too, will face continuing changes while ultimately having to stay much the same as he is today.

I joined the Army in February of 1963 and became a medic on a Special Forces A-Team. In the early 1980s I transferred to military intelligence support. During these three decades, from the draft era to today's volunteer Army, I have seen extensive changes, in both soldiers and equipment. I have seen these changes from the perspective of both combat units and combat support units and have formed my opinions about the real "professional soldier."

Today's soldier is still in the business of waging war. He is much more than just a fighter. He is often also a scholar and technician. He is not perfect. What I don't see in today's soldier is the passion—joining the Army to fight for a heroic cause. What I do see are young officers and enlisted soldiers who join the Army for reasons almost totally self-centered. They need money for school. They need a job, or face pressure from a family where service is a tradition. They dropped out of school with no place to go, or go to military schools for future civilian jobs. Few today join to be professional soldiers.

Some of these "soldiers" mature beyond short-term personal gain and ego. Confident in their own ability, they are willing to support the needs and mission of the Army no matter where it might lead. They become the true professionals, the very small but indispensable corps that holds the rest of the Army together. Every unit has those few officers and soldiers who always manage to get the job done or solve the problems that seem to be beyond the rest. Everyone who has ever served in the Army will remember those few soldiers who always got called on because they would do the job right. They also remember the few senior NCOs and officers who stood out as real leaders—honest, capable, and caring. They often did not stand out as exceptionally gung ho; they just quietly saw what needed doing and did it.

One of the continuing changes I have seen is in the relationship of the roles of officers and NCOs. As the officer becomes more a strategist and a manager of resources, such as manpower, material, and money, the NCO will become more a trainer, evaluator, and tactician. As the role of the officer becomes increasingly managerial, the success of the combat soldier will depend more and more on the few good NCOs.

Officers are assuming expanding roles and are becoming a new breed of managers. They are often responsible for maintaining and ensuring the support of multimillion dollar inventories and incredible firepower. Their communication and coordination skills will become even more critical as multi-unit and even multinational task forces become the standard combat organization. Even company grade officers must become involved with budget management.

Some traditional roles are becoming increasingly difficult for officers. They are responsible for evaluating the training and combat status of the soldiers below them, often with little knowledge of the soldier's specific skills. In most branches of the service it is highly unusual for an officer to have the technical knowledge of his subordinates. He may have an overview to give him a basic understanding of the soldier's capabilities, but there is a big difference between *knowing about* a subject and *knowing* the subject. It is not too hard for a

Ranger-trained infantry officer to evaluate the combat skills of his assigned infantry soldiers, but how does an average officer determine the skill level of an electronics technician, an Arabic linguist, or any of the high-tech positions on which the Army has become dependant for support?

The Army has for years tried to develop tests that would give the commanders this evaluation tool—the MOE test, the EQT, and now the SDT. The constant changes in the test itself suggests the failure of testing as an adequate measure of skill or ability. I believe that NCOs, as technicians, are better qualified to determine individual ability levels and training requirements and will eventually do this skill evaluation.

The chain of command rates NCOs on their job performance at least annually. I think that the NCOER will become the primary evaluation tool and the SDT (and its like) a bureaucratic and statistical tool. I have always found the dual evaluations somewhat curious. If the soldier receives an excellent NCOER for his job performance, who genuinely cares how he does on the EQT or SDT? It may show the need for increased emphasis in training, but little if any adverse action will be taken. If the soldier has earned a poor NCOER due to a lack of demonstrated ability or poor attitude, no favorable action will be taken even if he scored well on the test.

As the services have become smaller and more competitive and the enlistment and promotion requirements have become higher, the educational differences between officers and NCOs have and will become less and less significant. An officer in the 1960s with four years of college and some leadership training was much more well rounded educationally to handle the challenge of command. He had the training to see a larger view of the Army than his enlisted subordinates, who often had less than an eighth-grade education (and sometimes were functionally illiterate). The ability to communicate was his biggest asset. Today, with most senior NCOs having at least two years of college, the difference in ability to communicate has almost ceased to exist. The educational differences between the officer corps and the NCO corps are becoming less and less distinct. It is no longer unusual to see an NCO with a postgraduate degree.

The relationship of the officer and the NCO should be that of a command team, united in goal and combining strengths and experience. The commander sets the mission or goal, the NCO sees that it gets done. Sadly, however, the relationships and roles of NCOs and officers can be strained and ill-defined. Among the hardest jobs for an NCO today is that of platoon sergeant. A senior NCO with ten to fifteen years of experience is responsible for helping to teach a lieutenant with less than two years time in service to be a future commander. Unfortunately, this NCO is also commanded by and rated by the junior officer, tempered somewhat by the senior rater, the company commander, who probably also has less time in the service than the NCO does.

The role of the NCO has always been that of a leader and a teacher, yet technology continues to increase the complexity of weapons systems, communications systems, and intelligence collection and dissemination systems. Computers are involved in almost everything except digging foxholes, and the task of the NCO to train leaders has become increasingly difficult. The technician soldier, at the lower-grade levels, has little opportunity to practice and learn leadership skills while doing his job and maintaining his technical training. In keeping with the Peter Principle, the technician who does his job well will get promoted, eventually to a leadership position, often with little more training than a month-long Primary Leadership

Development Course. A fortunate new NCO will have an environment where he will have a mentor and learn to become one of the few good leaders. Unfortunately, the majority will learn on their own to survive well enough to get by and, someday retire without having done too much damage.

The Army is changing, has always changed, and will continue to evolve. The warrior is also evolving. A good backwoodsman had most of the skills needed to be a warrior in the Civil War. Today, even the best of the warriors are dependent to a much greater degree on a team effort. Teamwork and interprofessional relationships are skills that are not easily learned or taught. The strength of a Special Forces A-Team is not based on the ability of any one individual, but rather in the combined strengths of the whole team. Each team member has unique skills and weaknesses. No one man is best in every skill. Team effort compensates for individual weaknesses.

The epic hero has no place on today's teams of warriors. The soldier who wants to be a star is apt to take actions based on his own ego gratification, often at the expense of the team effort. This does not preclude heroic acts in support of the team. The hero of today stars in the background of a team effort, often overlooked and unrecognized, but secure in his own knowledge that he did his best and did what was right.

The traits of the professional haven't changed, but the emphasis must be on building teams while developing future NCOs. The following are some of the elements that will become increasingly important:

1. *Education.* The ability to write and communicate is invaluable. The NCO must be able to articulate problems and to suggest solutions.
2. *The ability to teach junior NCOs.* Junior NCOs must have

a mentor and the environment in which to learn and grow in their abilities, even when that opportunity guarantees that mistakes will be made. The mistakes must be allowed and then used as a teaching tool so that the young NCO will learn not only that he erred, but also why, what the effects were, and how to prevent like occurrences in the future.

3. *Honesty and integrity.* There is no possibility of strong teamwork without total trust and respect. There is no such thing as a "white lie." There is no requirement in the charter for an NCO that says he must be a "gentleman." Tell it like it is.

4. *Professionalism.* There is no room for personality conflicts with the professional. The NCO must discipline himself to put personal likes and dislikes into perspective with every decision. Likes and dislikes do not correlate with right and wrong. Anger is a weakness; high blood pressure and vocal outbursts express dissatisfaction, but they don't find solutions or prevent recurrences.

5. *Flexibility.* Every soldier and every mission is different. The NCO must be prepared to adapt to changing environments and must be willing to train every new soldier, regardless of background, into an effective soldier.

6. *Courage.* Be morally strong enough to make the hard decisions. If a soldier can be trained to be successful, train him; if not, eliminate him from the service.

7. *Confidence.* Micro-management at any command level suggests a lack of trust, an inability to delegate authority, and an attempt to prevent the judgment or actions of others from reflecting on oneself. The greatest failing in micro-management is that there is no depth of training or authority. The micro-manager will sometimes be absent

or leave for a new job. He has not prepared the subordinates left behind to make the correct decisions or take responsibility. He effectively hamstrings the progress of his unit. It's easy to do things yourself; it's not so easy to let others make mistakes for you, and then take the blame.

In the smaller high-tech Army of the future, the need for the few professional soldiers will be harder and harder to fill. As the required qualifications increase, the number of those able to meet them decreases. It is hoped there will always be enough of the few leaders, the true warriors, who always do whatever it takes to get the job done.

The more things change, the more they stay the same. The role of the future NCO in a changing Army will be no different from today: Accomplish the mission, take care of the troops.

Cpt. Mitchell Burnside Clapp

PRECISION AND MORALITY

When the first tribes went to war, there was no question who the combatants were: the other people with weapons who were swinging them at you. There was scant chance of bringing a weapon to bear against someone whom there was no quarrel, because the reach of a weapon was little more than the reach of a strong right arm. Over the years, though, the distinction between combatants and noncombatants has become blurred. As the power of man's weapons has grown, his ability to control them has been hard pressed. By World War II, one nation, the United States, was able to drop over two million tons of bombs on Axis forces, but half of them fell farther than 3,300 feet from the target. In the nuclear bombings of Hiroshima and Nagasaki, many important strategic targets were destroyed, but over 130,000 people lost their lives, of whom very few were enemy soldiers. War should, of course, never be entered lightly, but this type of war, where the majority of the killed and wounded are civilians, is especially difficult to justify.

In the 1970s and 1980s, the military significance of precision has been questioned. Some military reformers have questioned the reliability and cost of smart munitions. In the early 1980s, the Union of Concerned Scientists attempted to compare the mutual threat posed by the Soviet and American strategic arsenals. They did this by dividing the yield of each warhead by its average mass distance, then adding the resulting numbers for each missile. The result was that the much more accurate American strategic missile force was perceived as more threatening than the larger Soviet force. If someone were to develop a single missile with the yield of a firecracker but perfect accuracy, then it would be perceived as infinitely threatening according to this scheme, despite the fact that it could be used against only one target. Nevertheless, much effort has been expended to develop highly accurate weapons, especially for tactical aircraft. Such weapons were used on a large scale in the Persian Gulf.

The Gulf War provides an excellent example of the value of precision weaponry. Although only 9 percent of the 84,000 tons of munitions the United States dropped on Iraqi forces were precision guided, it accounted for a major portion of the total damage inflicted on the enemy, especially for difficult, hardened targets such as command bunkers. Although stealth, training, and superb airlift and aerial refueling support played a major role in the coalition victory, the effect of precision weapons was decisive in this conflict and illustrates the importance of smart munitions for future wars involving air power.

Precision weaponry first made its mark in the Southeast Asia conflict when a bridge in North Vietnam, which had survived conventional bombing for many years, finally succumbed to a single laser-guided bomb. In Iraq and Kuwait, smart bombs went much further. First of all, the ability to inflict strikes of high accuracy at will anywhere in the country offset the military principal of mass. Fewer sorties were required to achieve the same military objectives, and any time enemy forces gathered in a single place, it became that much easier for coalition aircraft to attack and destroy them. Rather than conferring an advantage, massing forces became a danger to the survival of those forces. Second, the accuracy of these weapons was better than anything that had been brought to the battlefield in the history of air power: an average of ten feet from the target, instead of the 3,300 feet in World War II. This gave one-weapon, one-kill capability against any pinpoint target, especially tanks. By the end of the war, Iraqi soldiers would not go near a tank at night because they kept exploding.

Smart bombs can achieve effects nearly as devastating as those of nuclear weapons with conventional munitions. Basically, every time the accuracy of a weapon is doubled, it is the same as increasing its yield eight-fold. Not only is this far less wasteful, but it reduces the risk to friendly forces, nearby areas, and especially to noncombatants. Visitors to Iraq following the conflict were surprised at the lack of damage to Iraqi houses, schools, and nonmilitary facilities. Yet the strikes against the command and control facilities, electrical power grid, and fuel and oil facilities left the enemy leadership blind, disoriented, ignorant, and paralyzed. Twelve hundred tons of bombs dropped in 500 sorties achieved a greater destructive effect against the Iraqi oil facilities than over 180,000 tons of bombs dropped in over 50,000 sorties against German oil facilities during World War II. And the amount of damage to Iraqi noncombatants and cultural and historical treasures was incomparably less than the damage to Germany after V-E day.

Consider, by contrast, the Iraqi Scud missile campaign, which illustrates the uselessness of imprecise weapons in achieving military objectives. Iraq launched 91 Scuds, of which 48 reached the target. About 450 people were wounded, 42 were killed, and around 10,000 buildings and homes were damaged or destroyed. This is an average of ten wounded, one killed, and 224 buildings damaged or destroyed per missile. The Germans did somewhat better in World War II with the V-2: 13 wounded, 5 killed, and 238 buildings per missile. Nearly all the casualties of the Scud campaign were innocents: civilians, noncombatant members of the coalition forces, and citizens of neutral countries such as Israel. Furthermore, the Scud campaign accomplished practically nothing of military value, destroying no important facilities or other significant targets.

The Scud campaign, however, illustrates an important limitation of precision weapons. It is imperative to be able to pinpoint the target. When the launch platform is mobile, it becomes very difficult to attack. Coalition forces in the Gulf War devoted nearly 2,500 sorties to finding and destroying Scud missiles. Despite these efforts, assisted by special forces on the ground, Iraqi missile launches were never completely neutralized. A reduction from five launches per day at the war's start to one per day at its conclusion was the best that could be achieved. Although the air campaign forced the Iraqis to launch their missiles in a hurry, and hence degraded their accuracy, mobile missiles posed a very difficult challenge, even with highly accurate weapons available. For similar reasons, it is easy to see how smart bombs may not be decisive against a low-level guerrilla enemy.

In conclusion, the advent of precision weaponry permits a new type of air war, capable of achieving strategic paralysis and selective destruction of military targets while keeping the injury to noncombatants at a minimum. As such, it is more morally justifiable, both because it reduces risk to friendly forces, and because it reduces risk to enemy civilians. If you believe that you have no business aiming a weapon at something you're not sure you can hit, then the case for precision weaponry becomes compelling.

Maj. William H. Burgess III:

"Special" operations are actions conducted by specially organized, trained, and equipped military and paramilitary forces to achieve military, political, economic, or psychological objectives by nonconventional military means in hostile, denied, or politically sensitive areas. Much of Special Operations entails selecting or otherwise identifying targets that cannot be attacked solely by general purpose (conventional) or strategic (nuclear) forces; formulating appropriate military responses (an amalgamation of forces, tactics, techniques, and procedures); and exercising selected responses. This dynamic aspect of the operational art of American Special Operations Forces, SOF, known simply as "targeting" among practitioners, is at the heart of Special Operations. SOF and Special Operations targeting will undergo remarkable development by increment and will quantum leap into the twenty-first century. Here, predictive discussion is premised on several assumptions:

- Change in targeting will result primarily from technological advance and political change.
- Technological advance will manifest itself primarily in

mobility, geometry, and interconnectivity of target sets, and in size, weight, durability, and utility of SOF equipment.

- The United States will continue to have vital national interests beyond its shores, particularly in the production and supply of strategic minerals and petroleum supplies.
- The United States will continue to maintain military force as an option when dealing with perceived threats to national interests.
- The military capabilities of the United States will be centered on a relatively small professional armed force operating within a strategy emphasizing power projection over forward defense.
- SOF will be used unilaterally in most situations below the threshold of war, and in situations of war or near-war as part of a larger package of quick-response contingency forces.
- Special operations targeting will be a subset of the activities of joint integrated "reconnaissance-strike complexes."
- Greater consequences of special operations targeting and associated activities will cause increased political employment and oversight of SOF.(SOF, along with some naval forces, have several advantages. in the eyes of political leaders, vis-a-vis the employment of general purpose forces: SOF are not perceived as "major combatants"; they can be employed without creating a national presence and commitment; and they can be withdrawn without major trauma.)

SOF will by the end of this century be established as a genuine operational-strategic arm, complementing the capabilities of other air, land, sea, and space forces and systems. SOF will not become a separate service in the twenty-first century, however. It is more probable that special operations capabilities will be tied to larger and more complex force modules, based in the continental United States. In fact, the economies possible through common support systems within a smaller overall force structure make it more likely that traditional service boundaries will atrophy and the United States will maintain SOF within a unified defense force, similar to the model of Canada, Israel, South Africa, and other nations.

The fundamental pattern of SOF employment in special reconnaissance, direct action, unconventional warfare, counterterrorism, and other missions will not change. SOF will continue to perform these functions for theater commanders and the National Command Authorities. The trend, however, will be toward vertical coordination at the joint, operational-strategic level with general purpose forces, and toward horizontal integration within SOF itself. The imperatives of maintaining relatively small armed forces with fewer assets while executing global contingency missions will promote a broader operational scope among American military organizations, such as may be witnessed in the ongoing evolution of attack helicopter capabilities within Army aviation. This, in turn, will narrow many distinctions between general purpose forces and SOF, and between the SOF of each service. Part of this trend will be habitual training and operational relationships between SOF and general purpose forces, e.g., between Special Forces battalions and airborne, air assault, and/or amphibious assault brigades that would deploy in sequence as expeditionary forces under a common theater operations plan. (OPLAN).

TARGET SELECTION

Special Operations targets will continue to be selected largely on the basis of national and theater objectives. Some target selection will be done within the context of established OP-LANs, while other selection will be "emergent" and based on either plans still in development or on short-fused contingencies. In the future, however, the character of many former special operations targets will change, and new types of targets will emerge. Technological advance and political factors will have particular impact on social infrastructure services and battlefield weapons systems, which will comprise the primary target sets for SOF in the next century.

Future battlefield weapons systems will become increasingly lethal (in terms of range and yield), mobile, agile, concealable, and available. Many targeted systems will become smaller, more diffuse, and redundant. As newer weapons systems are produced and introduced, older systems will displace to other nations. By the middle of the century, a large number of unstable and/or belligerent nations will possess fixed and mobile intermediate-range ballistic missile (IRBM) systems capable of carrying domestically produced nuclear, biological, or chemical warheads thousands of miles from their launch sites. These systems and their components will become harder to find and fix by standard technical means, and their threatened use will entail more compressed response times. New operational-strategic target systems will also emerge in the form of advanced ground- and space-based weapons and weapons support systems. Particle-beam air defense guns, electromagnetic pulse generators, ground-launched anti-satellite missile systems, and other such weaponry will complement, and to a degree replace, precision weapons and weapons of mass destruction. These new systems will also comprise technologically advanced and (from the SOF perspective) fragile command and control nodes, such as satellite ground control stations, that will in and of themselves become special operations targets.

International society will become increasingly integrated and interdependent on fewer, more expensive, and vulnerable high-technology macrosystems for energy, communications, transportation, information, and industrial activities. Specialized manufacturing processes associated with such macrosystems, especially those utilizing strategic minerals, will become increasingly elegant and transnational in character. Such macrosystems and their supporting manufacturing processes will present a narrower array of potential targets (and fewer "Achilles heel" target components) to concentrate on, with greater effects for relatively less effort.

In some states, for example, base load electric power generating stations will become larger in output and fewer in number, providing power to larger numbers of consumers spread over wider geographic areas. Telecommunications utilities will become multinational in components and functions, particularly in linguistically and culturally homogeneous regions such as Latin America. The potential effects of Special Operations targeting against such macrosystems will thus become more expansive and pervasive, with far greater political implications and consequences than was possible in the 20th century.

FORMULATING RESPONSE

Technological advance will impact on organization, weapons, equipment, methods of attack, and other elements that frame specific responses to Special Operations targeting problems.

194

Tailored data collection and applications of interactive artificial intelligence in planning and execution will allow SOF to "see" their objectives with greater precision, significantly reducing uncertainty and risk at all stages of operations. Enhanced mobility, sustainment, and communications systems will give SOF unprecedented reach, staying power, survivability, and responsiveness, although hostile countermeasures are likely to be enhanced in comparable ways.

SOF will be able to move against targets on shorter notice. They will have the capability to move more quickly and deeply into, around, and out of denied or contested territory, e.g., through the use of ultra-lights, tilt-rotor aircraft, all-terrain vehicles, and inflatable submersibles. SOF will provide and be provided with higher quantity and quality of real-time information during operations as through the use of secure miniature video cameras interfaced with hand-size VHF/satellite communications radio-telephones.

Technological advance will also promote further integration of SOF into operational-strategic reconnaissance-strike complexes, in which SOF will provide pre-strike reconnaissance and surveillance, target acquisition, and post-strike assessment for theater deep-strike weapons systems. Hostile weaponry that offsets the effectiveness of technology-based weapons systems will have to be targeted by human-based systems such as SOF in an asymmetrical application of force. Instead of direct assault against the hardened and well-defended weapons themselves, SOF will more likely perform pre-strike reconnaissance and surveillance, target acquisition (e.g., the "marking" of targets via laser designation) for air and or missile strikes, and post-strike assessment. SOF direct assault will more likely go after "softer" supporting systems and personnel to capture components, equipment, and expertise for purposes of technical intelligence exploitation, or destroy or eliminate such.

The future means by which SOF will locate and attack its targets will incorporate several technological advances. When conducting target detection and acquisition, SOF will use a variety of sensor systems that will permit it to find and track its targets by magnetic, seismic, radiological, audio, and olfactory means, even where the target is beneath the earth. SOF will use high-kinetic-energy rifle and pistol projectiles, and smart indirect fire weapons rounds that can "fly" and seek preprogrammed targets, such as specific vehicles in a convoy. SOF will also employ enhanced hand action, e.g., through explosives that can be applied as liquids or shapeable solids, binary petroleum contaminants, metal embrittlement, harmonic degradation, and the like. Demographic and political change, however, will exert an increasingly restrictive force on Special Operations in situations short of overt warfare. There will be relatively few underdeveloped places in the world by the middle of the twenty-first century. With rising economic and social interdependencies, nationalism and/or regionalism will make nations more assertive and less inclined to support military intervention by outside forces, either in their own territories or in the territories of neighboring states. At the same time, however, competition among nations for natural resources will intensify, as will security interests tied to the uninterrupted supply of such resources.

Another restrictive factor influencing SOF will be that, within a few decades, most people in the developed countries will live on urbanized terrain. With increasing social centralization, more Special Operations targets will be found in or near cities and towns. Also, most countries and regions will have well-developed police, paramilitary, and military forces to control populated areas and defend critical targets. Where these areas are denied or contested, Special Operations will likely emphasize target detection and acquisition for smart and precision-guided weaponry. There will still be a large mission outside of urban areas, but Special Operations targeting is likely to become somewhat more urban-based and place greater emphasis on the use of indigenous surrogates.

International arms limitation agreements of the future will increasingly circumscribe the use of weapons of mass destruction and attendant long-range delivery systems. SOF or SOF-like forces will therefore gain an enhanced role in the pursuit of specific political and military objectives as an alternative to more conspicuous and potentially escalatory means. National policy makers will increasingly want to use Special Operations below the trip-wire of conventional warfare, although such use will not necessarily be primarily "black," or covert.

As national political implications of Special Operations increase, Congressional oversight will expand and intensify. Lending additional impetus to increased oversight will be an aversion among senior military leaders and members of Congress to the cult of black operations, intensified over time by occasional but seemingly inevitable scandals revealing the use of "cover" more to conceal improprieties and escape accountability than to deceive foreign enemies. (This will be offset to a degree, however, as SOF increases training, professionalism, self-identity, and willingness to cull malefactors from its ranks.) The end result will be that the efficacy of special operations will increasingly be subject to the checks and balances of the democratic process and the scrutiny of elected officials.

CONCLUSION

Special Operations will remain a human-based, and at times personality-driven, activity to the end of the next century.

197

Human capabilities will be greatly enhanced by technology, but there will be an inherent danger that the technical aspects of Special Operations targeting will come to override its human aspects. A tendency toward such may be seen in the vulnerability some in the SOF community have to the siren's call of artificial intelligence, robotics, and various other technology that displaces reason and makes humans merely monitors and not masters of their tools. Another danger is that the ethical constraints on Special Operations targeting may not always keep pace with technology or will be weakened by exigent political factors, and Special Operations will be undertaken in ways that are at variance with democratic ideals. If these and other dangers can be overcome, however, the twenty-first century will be an era of historical achievement for American SOF.

Col. John Warden III

THINKING ACROSS HISTORICAL DISCONTINUITIES

Since 1989, we have lived through more revolutionary changes than has any generation throughout recorded history. Dealing with such dramatic change is exceedingly difficult. For all our lives and for countless generations of our ancestors, the world has been one in which multiple powers of roughly equal strength fought each other for regional or global domination. Today, the United States dominates the world as no state has since Rome.

For the last hundred years, mass production has been the key to economic—and military—success; today, mass production is as antiquated as the craft guilds it replaced.

For thousands of years, success in war meant killing more of

198

the enemy than the enemy was willing to tolerate. In 1991, the United States and its coalition partners defeated an entire nation with very few casualties on either side. They did this by selectively destroying the relative handful of facilities and weapons without which Iraq could not wage war or even defend itself.

We have seen three revolutions in the last few years—and all our old rules in warfare, economics, and international relations need rewriting.

These are heady ideas—which necessarily produce heady questions that demand answers. Do we want to maintain military dominance of the world? If we do want to remain dominant, what should our force structure look like? When a dominant power fights—albeit for objectives well less than national survival—does it fight differently than it would have in the old world? Aside from the political issues, does the revolution in warfare suggest a significantly new approach to war and to force structure? We won't try to answer these questions directly, but we will try to make the nature of the military revolution a little clearer so that we have a basis for addressing the more encompassing questions.

If we have passed through a revolution, it is imperative that we think in revolutionary terms. Otherwise we are doomed to the same kinds of defeat that has afflicted armies and navies which have refused to recognize changes far less than those we have just witnessed. Unfortunately, human nature, parochialism, and innate conservatism make thinking across a historical discontinuity the most difficult of tasks. To begin the very hard but very necessary process of thinking in revolutionary terms, we must understand the real implications of what happened in the Gulf.

We can identify ten concepts that summarize the revolution

of the Gulf War and which must be taken into account as we develop new force levels and strategy:

1. The importance of strategic attack and the fragility of states at the strategic level of war
2. Fatal consequences of losing strategic air superiority
3. The overwhelming effects of parallel warfare
4. The value of precision weapons
5. The fragility of surface forces at the operational level
6. Fatal consequences of losing operational air superiority
7. Stealth and precision together redefine mass and surprise
8. The viability of "air occupation"
9. The dominance of air power
10. Air, sea, and ground components contribute the most when they are directed as discrete elements

The importance of strategic attack and the fragility of states at the strategic level of war. Countries are inverted pyramids that rest precariously on their strategic innards—their leadership, communications, key production, infrastructure, and population. If a country is paralyzed strategically, it is defeated and cannot sustain its fielded forces, though they be fully intact. The idea of a country without an army is easy to grasp; the idea of an army without a country is an absurdity.

The importance of the strategic base has been clear to smart leaders since the earliest days. Alexander understood it in terms of preparing his own base before he set off to conquer Persia, and he understood the necessity to deny his enemy the support of his own base. For Alexander and most who followed him up to this century, however, the only way to get at the strategic base of the enemy was through defeat of the enemy's army—

200

the entity that existed first and foremost to protect the strategic base. Given this situation, the strategic base looked like the bottom half of a very stable pyramid—in other words, it was not vulnerable except by chipping away at it from the top—the army point—down. The exception to the general rule in the past came in states heavily dependent on the sea for food or wealth; in these circumstances, an enemy could prevail by stopping sea movement of necessities. The efficacy of this approach, in the limited areas where it pertained, has been clear from the days of ancient Athens right through the blockade of Germany after the Armistice in 1918.

In this century, the vulnerability of the strategic base began to change. We saw the first demonstrations in the aerial attacks against Germany and Japan, which clearly had a major effect, but whose effect was easy to confuse with other factors. In the Gulf War, the fragility of the state at the strategic level became crystal clear.

All states look about the same at the strategic level. As an example, all have one or two people at the top with a dozen or so cabinet members under them. Each cabinet member has a half-dozen or so sub-cabinet members. A small state may have no more layers, a large state may have several more. Below about the third layer, however, the knowledge and authority of individuals is so limited that they cannot plan or execute strategic operations in defense of offense. Thus, paralyzing the first three layers, common to every country, imposes a paralysis in leadership. The same concepts of distribution appear in communications (think about the number of regional switching centers in the United States), transportation, power production, and other strategic centers upon which a nation utterly depends.

In the past, of course, reaching strategic centers was only

201

possible after normally arduous defeat of the enemy army defending them. In World War II, aerial bombardment worked, but only after along effort and high cost. The basic problem was one of accuracy; small things, which are the essence of strategic centers of gravity, were difficult to destroy when the average bomb fell over three thousand feet from where it was aimed. As we know the average bomb dropped in the Gulf War by precision capable platforms like the F-117 and the F-111F fell within three feet of its target.

Fatal consequences of losing strategic air superiority. When a state loses its ability to protect itself from air attack, it is at the mercy of its enemy, and only the enemy's compassion or exhaustion can save it. The first reason for the existence of government is to protect the citizenry and its property. When a state can no longer do so, it has lost its reason for being. When a state loses strategic air superiority and has no reasonable hope of regaining it quickly, it should sue for peace as quickly as possible. From an offensive standpoint, winning strategic air superiority is the number one priority of the commander; once accomplished, everything else is just a matter of time.

The overwhelming effects of parallel warfare. States have a number of vital targets at the strategic level—in the neighborhood of a few hundred, with an average of perhaps ten aimpoints per vital target. These targets tend to be small, very expensive, have few backups, and are hard to repair. If a significant percentage are struck in parallel, the damage becomes insuperable. Contrast parallel attack with serial attack, where only one or two targets come under attack in a given day (or longer): The enemy can alleviate the effects of serial attack by dispersal over time, increasing the defenses of targets that are likely to be attacked, concentrating resources to repair damage to single targets, and by conducting counteroffensives. Parallel attack deprives the enemy of the ability to respond effectively, and the greater the percentage of targets hit in a single blow, the more nearly impossible is response.

Parallel attack has not been possible on any appreciable scale in the past because a commander had to concentrate his forces in order to prevail against a single vulnerable part of the enemy's forces. If he prevailed, he could reconcentrate and move on to attack another point in the enemy's defenses. The process of concentrating and reconcentrating was normally lengthy and one that the enemy worked hard to foil. This process, better understood when labeled *serial warfare,* permitted maneuver and countermaneuver, attack and counterattack, and movement and pause. It also gave rise to the phenomenon known as the *culminating point* in campaigns— that point at which the campaign is in near equilibrium, where the right effort on either side can have significant effect. All our thinking on war is based on serial effects, on ebb and flow. The capability to execute parallel war, makes that thinking obsolete.

Technology has made possible the near simultaneous attack on every strategic- and operational-level vulnerability of the enemy. This parallel process of war, as opposed to the old serial form makes very real what Clausewitz called the ideal form of war, the striking of blows everywhere at the same time. For Clausewitz, the ideal was a Platonian shadow on the back of the cave wall, never to be known by mortals. The shadow has materialized and nothing will be the same again.

The value of precision weapons. Precision weapons allow the economical destruction of virtually all targets—especially strategic and operation targets that are difficult to move or conceal.

203

They change the nature of war from one of probability to one of certainty. Wars for millennia have been probability events where each side launched huge quantities of projectiles (and men) at one another in the hope that enough of the projectiles (and men) would kill enough to induce the other side to retreat or surrender. Probability warfare was chancy at best. It was unpredictable, full of surprise, hard to quantify, and governed by accident. Precision weapons have changed all that. In the Gulf War, we knew with near certainty that a single weapon would destroy its target. War moved into the predictable.

With precision weapons, even logistics becomes simple: destruction of the Iraqis at the strategic, operational, and tactical levels required about twelve thousand aimpoints be hit. Thus, no longer is it necessary to move a near infinite quantity of munitions so that some tiny percentage might hit something important. Since the Iraqi army was the largest fielded since the Chinese in the Korean War and since we know that all countries look about the same at the strategic and operational level, we can forecast in advance how many precision weapons will be needed to defeat an enemy—assuming of course that we are confident about getting the weapons to their target.

The fragility of surface forces at the operational level. Supporting significant numbers of surface forces is a tough administrative problem, even in peacetime. Success depends upon efficient distribution of information, fuel, food, and ammunition. By necessity, efficient distribution depends on an inverted pyramid of distribution. Supplies of all operational commodities must be accumulated in one or two locations, then passed out to two or four locations, and so on until they eventually reach the user. The nodes in the system are exceptionally vulnerable to precision attack. As an example, consider what the effect would have been of a single air raid a day—even with non-precision weapons—on the WWII Red Ball Express or on the buildup behind VII and XVIII Corps in the Gulf War. The Redball Express became internally unsustainable, and the VII and XVIII Corps buildups severely strained the resources of the entire U.S. Army.

Logistics and administration dominate surface warfare, and neither is easy to defend. In the past, these activities took place so far behind the lines that they were reasonably secure. Such is no longer the case—which brings into serious question any form of warfare that requires huge logistic and administrative buildup.

Fatal consequences of losing operational air superiority.

Functioning at the operational level is difficult even without enemy interference. If the enemy attains operation air superiority and can roam at will above indispensable operational functions like supply, communications, and movement, success is not possible. As with the loss of strategic air superiority, loss of operational air superiority spells doom and should prompt quick measures to retreat—which is likely to be very costly—or to arrange for surrender terms.

Stealth and precision together redefine mass and surprise.

For the first time in the history of warfare, a single entity can produce its own mass and surprise. It is this single entity that makes parallel warfare possible. Surprise has always been one of the most important factors in war—perhaps even the single most important because it could make up for large deficiencies in numbers. Surprise was always difficult to achieve, because it conflicted with the concepts of mass and concentration. In order to have enough forces available to hurl enough projectiles to win the probability contest, a commander had to assemble and move large numbers. Of course, assembling and moving large forces in secret was quite difficult, even in the days before aerial reconnaissance, so the odds on surprising the enemy were small indeed. Stealth and precision have solved both sides of the problem; by definition, stealth achieves surprise, and precision means that a single weapon accomplishes what thousands were unlikely to accomplish in the past.

The viability of "air occupation."   Countries conform to the will of their enemies when the penalty for not conforming exceeds the cost of conforming. "Cost" can be imposed on a state by paralyzing or destroying its strategic and operational base or by actual occupation of enemy territory. In the past, occupation (in the rare instances when it was needed or possible) was accomplished by ground forces—because there was no good substitute. Today, the concept of "air occupation" is a reality, and in many cases it will suffice. The Iraqis are conforming as much or more with UN demands, as the French did with German demands when occupied by millions of Germans. Ground occupation, however, is indicated when the intent is to colonize or otherwise appropriate the enemy's homeland.

The dominance of air power.   Air power (fixed wing, helicopter, cruise missile, satellite), if not checked, will destroy an enemy's strategic and operational target base—which are very vulnerable and very difficult to make less vulnerable. It can also destroy most tactical targets if necessary. Air power may not be dominant forever, but it is as dominant over surface forces as the phalanx was over the mob, as the rifle and cannon were over the heavy knight, as barbed wire and the machine gun were against the infantry charge, as steamships were over sailing ships. Each of these had their day in the sun only to see the sun finally set. That the sun finally set, however, didn't deny their dominance, however short-lived.

It only makes sense to build battle and campaign plans around the dominant force. To do otherwise is folly.

Air, sea, and ground components contribute the most when they are directed as discrete elements. Sailors know how to organize and undertake sea operations, soldiers know how to move forces on the ground, and airmen know how to employ force through the air. They derive the needed expertise through long years of practice. It is illogical to deny each the opportunity to put his component to the best use in support of theater objectives. There is an air campaign, a sea campaign, and a ground campaign. They are as unique, one from another, as are the eagle, the shark, and the tiger. Which one is the "key force," the most important to attainment of a particular objective, will depend on the objective.

Nothing could be less "joint" than to say that air and sea power must always support ground power, or that ground power is the key force in every situation. Once a key force is identified to fit the particular situation, the other forces must be orchestrated to complement the key force. Orchestration is not the same as integration.

For the next quarter- to half-century, air power will frequently be the key force because it will dominate most operational and strategic level combats—but not all. Air power is useless to solve a Panama or Grenada situation where the bad must be carefully sorted from the good. Some phases of a war, even where air power is dominant overall, can only be addressed by surface power. For example, to the extent that it was necessary to put a prompt halt to Iraqi atrocities in Kuwait at the end of February, only a ground attack could promise a quick end.

The revolution has happened and we must deal with it—not ignore it. It is human nature to stay with the old ways of doing business even when the external world has made the old ways obsolete or even dangerous. So many examples come easily to mind: the heavy knights at Agincourt refusing to believe that they were being destroyed by peasants with bows; the French in World War I exulting in the doctrine of "cold steel" against the machine gun and barbed wire as the flower of a generation perished; and the steel and auto makers of the United States convinced that their foreign competitors were inept even as their market positions plummeted. Accepting the changes made manifest in the Gulf War will be equally difficult for the United States.

Fortunately, our overwhelming superiority means we can do anything, no matter how shortsighted, without serious danger in the next decade. After that, however, we can be assured that our enemies will have learned from us and will strive to become superior to us in the air. They will recognize the futility of massing armies; they will recognize that the world has passed from the age of mass to the age of precision, from the age of probability to the age of certainty. We can't fault the Iraqis for the way they planned to conduct the war; their battle plans and assumptions were not much different from our plans and assumptions for the great war on the Fulda Gap. They could hardly know that we would fight in an entirely new way, that we would base our war plans on air power, and that we would refuse to fight them man to man as we had always done. The Iraqis can be excused for lack of prescience; if we fail to change, however, it will not be for our inability to know the future, but for our inability to understand the recent past.

Editors' comment:

Colonel John Warden III speaks of historical discontinuities that must be mentally overcome by leaps of understanding. Such leaps are difficult for the people whose job it is to work day after day at a compartmentalized set of tasks designed to work in a world that may only seem to be the same as it ever was.

The progress of our bureaucracy toward new methodologies is excruciatingly slow. Our system of government was purposely designed to be resistant to abrupt change. At the time of the Founding Fathers, this was a safety precaution, but now this lugubrious nature of our huge and bloated bureaucracy may be more dangerous than any of us fully comprehend. The swift acceleration of political and technological events, when added to this inherent inability to react quickly, may create an additional discontinuity between our policy makers views of reality and reality itself.

Bureaucrats, like any other endangered species, react to threats to their survival by fighting back. For example, if the international arms control institutions of the world are threatened by a reduction in nuclear forces, which would in turn demand a reduction in the forces of arms control experts, then their reaction may be to try to reinstate the status quo ante, up to and including the bipolar world.

So we must be on our guard against not only wrong action, but also wrong reaction and wrong inaction. All of our futures depend on this peculiarly modern sort of vigilance, made possible by the technological triumphs of the very bureaucracy whose survival is now threatened by its own accomplishments.

The Overachievers

In this section you will find sixteen questions with the answers of six contributers grouped beneath each question. The questions are presented in the same order in which they appeared on the original questionnaire, thereby giving the reader a chance to have an experience similar to that of the contributors and to gain any extra insight derived from considering the questions as a Gestalt.

We have chosen to separate these six contributors and group them in this section for several reasons. Although many other contributors answered a large number of questions, these answered all, or nearly all. We had carefully not required that respondents answer all the questions. We did not, however, expressly forbid the prodigious effort that such a response would take. When we received the first response answering all questions, we considered it a fluke: the writer had scribbled short answers between the lines of the questionnaire. We assumed it was an off-handed response, just short of no response at all, since the author hadn't bothered to type, double-space, or do any more than was absolutely necessary.

We held the piece back, intending to discard it as being insufficiently considered and therefore not illuminating. Then we got a second response, this one more seriously composed, but still written on the form by hand, in between the lines. We looked again at our page of directions and decided that perhaps we hadn't been clear. If one decided to answer all or nearly all the questions, in order to keep those answers under the 2,000-word ceiling, one would necessarily need to be terse.

When we received the third response of this sort, it was from an extremely desirable respondent, and we took yet another look at the two earlier pieces we had received. At that moment, we decided to run the three pieces under "The Overachievers" title and give this type of response its own category, since we were clearly dealing with a subset of respondents who just couldn't resist trying to run the entire gamut of questions.

It's a good thing we allowed nature to take its course. The Overachievers contains the responses of six authors to sixteen questions from the original questionnaire, and the roundtable that develops by printing the questions and responses in series is a dialogue we're especially pleased to present as a final chapter to this exploration of the nature of the American warrior.

Following are the six overachievers who participated:

Mark Barent
Steve Hartov
Col. William P. Schneider
Brig. Gen. John F. Stewart, Jr.
Charles E. Thompson
Lt. Commander Michael Walsh

Warriorship

1. Are warriors made, or born?

BARENT: Born.

HARTOV: The warrior element is genetic. However, the growth environment is the determining factor. A woman who becomes a helicopter pilot for the U.S. Army, given an identical growth environment in Sweden, might well become a doctor.

SCHNEIDER: They are made.

STEWART: The absolutely great ones are born. The rest of us are made.

THOMPSON: Both. Most, but not all, people can be "made" into warriors.

WALSH: I believe that I was born to this life. I can imagine no other where the challenges are as great. Nothing really worth having is easy, and the only easy day was yesterday.

2. Describe the qualities that a warrior must have to survive and prevail.

BARENT: Courage and Integrity.

HARTOV: This may seem odd, but I believe that a true warrior must possess a certain talent for self-deception, for as all martial artists know, one must be able to perceive victory where none is possible in order to be victorious. Certainly on the modern-day battlefield the ability to suppress the imagination is critical, for if a warrior allows the lethal realities to impose upon the psyche, then he or she would be immobilized. Certainly all of the cliché values of duty, honor, and country must be inherent, for a belief in "the cause" is a requisite before one can even begin to become a warrior.

SCHNEIDER: Independence of thought, but with willingness to subordinate his actions to the desires of his commanders. Good health. Tenacity. Patience. Intelligence.

STEWART: Intelligence, leadership ability to overcome failures, calmness, vision, compassion, caring, empathy, and decisiveness.

WALSH: Shoot, move, think, communicate, and survive.

3. What are the emotional rewards of warriorship?

BARENT: Didn't know I was a warrior. Never thought about it. Emotional reward of military service was camaraderie.

HARTOV: Enduring the hardships of an elite unit is in itself rewarding, giving the individual great self-confidence and emotional resilience. However, there is also a certain sense of pride in knowing that you are prepared to fight and perhaps die for a conviction.

SCHNEIDER: The primary rewards of warriorship is the knowledge that you have led a group of your fellow citizens in the defense of your country, and probably saved many of their lives by virtue of your leadership, and earned the respect of your fellow citizens for the job you have done.

STEWART: Satisfaction of being part of the Army serving the best country. Working with dedicated Americans.

THOMPSON: At first it was the sense of "freedom" I experienced at being (more or less) on my own. This was followed closely by a sense of achievement in my ability to handle the hardships of military life and function well in that environment. Later, I discovered that the real reward for finishing flight training wasn't the "Wings of Gold" pinned on my chest, but the enormous golden ego that went with it. Not only had I attempted a feat that the vast majority of the American population avoided, but I had succeeded where many of those who did attempt the feat had failed. I still feel that way. Finally, military service is an honorable profession, perhaps the most honorable of any in America. As a result, I believe myself an honorable man and this is perhaps the greatest reward of all.

WALSH: This is a tough question. *True* warriors do not usually associate emotion with pure warriorship. Emotion is there, of course, but in the Special Warfare business, it had better be below the surface. I believe the rewards of warriorship are in the skills one develops and perfects over the years, and the pride that comes from doing them well. Warriorship is also learning to deal with fear—your own fears, your deepest, darkest fears—and dealing with all that. This is especially true in the Navy SEAL business, as our business is the very unforgiving environment of water. When you must swim underneath a ship at night in January, and you are avoiding everything that can hurt you, like a sea induction, you must have self-control and confidence. This is what being a Navy SEAL is all about—finding out who you really are, and dealing with that realistically.

4. **All successful warriors subscribe to an ethic of behavior, a code of honor. Some call this "common values" and others say it is a "sense of duty." Say what warriorship means to you. How do you see your role in society?**

BARENT: To perform my duty to the best of my ability.

HARTOV: True warriorship has nothing to do with uni-forms, medals, polished boots, or a strutting posture. It is a quiet practise encompassing all of those simple values from "fair play" to "sense of commitment," with a willingness to perform distasteful acts from a sense of duty rather than desire. Unlike the manner in which many societies view their soldiers, I do not see my role as that of the hired guard dog protecting life and property. Instead, I see the role as that of the father to his family.

SCHNEIDER: Duty—an understanding of what is right and willingness to do it no matter what. Honor—personal integrity. *I say, I do*—as the old English knight had engraved on his escutcheon. Country—I have sworn to defend the Constitution—when my constitutional leaders give me a legal order I must execute it, at peril of my life if need be. My role in society was to defend it with my body and mind—now with my mind since they don't want my body anymore.

STEWART: Higher standards of honesty, dedication, technical proficiency. Serve when and where called. Forge teams and care for individuals. Overcome odds and prevail. Give to a higher calling.

THOMPSON: Warriorship means that the warrior is willing to put others before himself. It is his or her duty to stand between his country and the rest of the world and, occasionally, advance his country's position in the world by force of arms. He or she is, in many instances, totally disgusted with the condition in the country, but believes that sooner or later the people will work out their own problems. The warrior's role is making sure that others, outside the country, don't interfere.

The military ethic is based on "service and selflessness." Were these characteristics more common in our society, I believe we'd have a better nation. I see my role as one that advances a sense of selflessness by personal

216

example. I wish I could do more, because I'm convinced that greed and selfishness and the general "me first" attitude demonstrated by most Americans is the root cause of our economic and social problems. I also believe that these will have some very bad, even fatal, results.

WALSH: Warriorship to me means that I am fulfilling my role in life. This is what God wants me to do. When He doesn't want me to do this anymore, He will let me know. My personal code is to remain loyal, remain alert and not fall asleep between wars, improve my skills, learn all I can, and be true to myself.

5. **Urban and guerilla warfare takes a special kind of warrior with special training. What have you learned through experience that would be most valuable to a young warrior training for this type of warfare today?**

BARENT: Learn now to trust first yourself then your partner.

HARTOV: Learn the language. It may seem simplistic, but language is the key to any culture, and when you understand the enemy's culture you can begin to think like him and, accordingly, defeat him. On short notice, this is of course impossible. However, in protracted conflicts it is an ideal focus.

SCHNEIDER: Urban warfare is just another form of warfare. Guerilla warfare presumes that you don't know who is friend or foe. Fight guerillas with guerilla tactics.

STEWART: Learn how to be an intelligence operator.

WALSH: There is a lot more to urban warfare than Close Quarter Combat skills. CQB is important, sure, but so is the rest of your skill bag. We need to remember that the chic, sexy ops are not the only show in town.

Personal Commitment

1. What is your most deeply held belief?

BARENT: That man can triumph over adversity.

HARTOV: That if one holds to the credo, "No retreat, no surrender," whether in the military or in everyday life, anything is possible.

SCHNEIDER: There is an afterlife.

STEWART: That this country is based on high ideals, institutionalized by our Constitution, and that it must be defended.

THOMPSON: That there is a God and that He has a plan for us. That this plan is totally beyond my comprehension is besides the point. That it is probably attached to the good we do during our lives is merely a wild guess on my part, but that guess is as good as any other.

WALSH: That there is a God, that Christ is really the Savior and that we are on the brink of the Second Coming. No question about it.

2. What single experience has most shaped your current beliefs?

BARENT: No one experience—there were several and they were all superb performances by people.

HARTOV: Managing to complete basic training in the Israeli Parachute Corps.

SCHNEIDER: Service on Okinawa, where I became convinced that I could no longer live as an atheist/agnostic.

STEWART: No single experience, an accumulation over the years.

THOMPSON: None that I can think of.

WALSH: There is no *singular* experience that I am aware of.

3. How, and why, did you initially enter the service of your country?

BARENT: To be a tail gunner on a B-29 in the Korean War.

HARTOV: Like many Israelis, I come from a background of persecution of Jews under Nazi Germany. My mother was a refugee, her family was virtually wiped out. Having U.S. citizenship in addition to Israeli, I did not have to serve in the IDF [Israel Defense Forces], but felt an obligation. I volunteered for service in the IDF parachute corps, much like Americans did in the RAF during WWII.

SCHNEIDER: I entered the USMA in the graduating class of 1946 on July 1, 1943, as a result of a Presidential appointment, after winning a competitive examination and passing a stringent physical examination, both at March Field, California. I had hoped to enter the Naval Academy as my father was a graduate of '17 and a career naval aviator, one of two to overfly the German High Seas Fleet in October 1918. He was also a heavier-than-air aircraft pilot on board the dirigible *Akron* before its untimely crash. I admired him immensely. There was a war going on and I wanted to defend my country.

STEWART: Through Army ROTC. I believe that every American should serve the U.S.A. I am deeply patriotic.

THOMPSON: I "ran away from home" and joined the Air Force as a way of going places and doing things I wouldn't be able to do otherwise.

WALSH: I joined the Navy in the spring of 1966 and entered active duty in Boston on 16 September. Since the earliest days I can remember I wanted to be in the military.

4. If you had the chance to change one thing you've done in your career, what would it be?

219

BARENT: Can't think of a thing.

HARTOV: I would have stayed in for the full twenty years and retired as a lieutenant colonel.

SCHNEIDER: I would not have driven to Carlsbad, New Mexico, in July of 1966. My wife was killed in an automobile wreck just outside of Carlsbad on the way back.

THOMPSON: I can't think of anything I'd change.

5. **If you hadn't become a warrior, what would you have done with your life?**

BARENT: Can't say.

HARTOV: I am now only a "part-time" warrior and am able to have the best of both worlds, which include a full family life and a profession as a writer.

SCHNEIDER: I never considered the question as a young man. It is too late now.

STEWART: Been a teacher or professor.

THOMPSON: I'd probably have been a teacher, social worker, or become a member of some other service-oriented profession.

WALSH: I don't even want to think about it.

6. **If you are no longer actively serving, how did your service shape your present career? Was it a plus or a minus? If you are actively serving, how do you expect your service to impact your future?**

BARENT: Definite plus.

HARTOV: I am now only an active reservist, but my military career has shaped every part of my civilian life. Warrior-ship gave me an inherent conviction that I could accomplish seemingly impossible objectives.

SCHNEIDER: My present activity is a continuation and an extension of my military service.

7. Do you feel estranged from the society you've sworn to serve or are you comfortable with your role? Why?

BARENT: Estranged, yes; comfortable, yes, because I stay away from them.

HARTOV: I am lucky in that the society I've sworn to serve embraces me without question. In Israel a professional warrior is considered at the highest social strata, for survival is a day-to-day issue.

SCHNEIDER: I am not estranged by my warriorness, but perhaps by my distaste for those who are trying to undermine family values.

STEWART: Very comfortable. The Army is a fine representation of American society.

WALSH: The military will always be somewhat estranged from the society it is sworn to protect. It has to be. The code that exists in the military is of a higher standard than that of society. Duty, Honor, Country are not household buzzwords in today's U.S. culture. To hold the total force together we need these higher standards. The country expects it of us, whether the grass roots American realizes it or not.

8. How does it feel to give orders that will clearly cause the deaths of some soldiers under your command? What advice do you have for those who must give such orders?

BARENT: Make damn sure they are correct and you yourself could carry them out.

HARTOV: Personally, it is an extremely uncomfortable feel-

221

ing. As an Airborne leader, even training situations involve putting my people at extreme risk, and I am never at ease and indeed suffer substantially until all are accounted for.

SCHNEIDER: I swore to obey the just and correct orders of my superiors; if those orders lead to death on the field of combat, that is unfortunate. My job is always to execute orders in such a way as to reduce casualties to the absolute minimum. I would counsel those who would give such orders to follow those precepts in good conscience.

STEWART: Try to minimize casualties constantly through thorough planning and through realistic training. Then, accomplish the mission.

WALSH: I did what was required tactically at the time. The fact that we were ambushed and most of us wounded and two killed is War, plain and simple. To those that follow, "Do the deed."

9. **What has it cost you, in human terms, to gather this expertise? How do you justify the personal cost? Do you feel that what you've accomplished has been worth the price you've paid? If you had it to do over again, would you join the warrior class?**

BARENT: 1. Not much. 2. Don't try. 3. Definitely. 4. Sure.

HARTOV: I confess that warriorship, because of the intensity of the transitional phase, has become something of an obsession. It pervades my everyday life, and I sometimes find myself unable to view situations from a less rigid perspective. However, the rewards far outweigh the detriments, and I would not trade my experiences for anything.

SCHNEIDER: This expertise was acquired while doing that which I considered to be my duty. It came with the turf.

Since the price was zero, any amount of benefit has to have had infinite value to me. Probably [do it over again].

STEWART: I've learned much, have had a wonderful life. I have financial security but gave up the chance to make real money. It's been worth it.

"THOMPSON: Although two of my three children have had a tough time adjusting to life, I can't say that warriorship, per se, is responsible for that. True, if I'd been home more, things may have been easier for them. But then again, maybe not. My marriage is failed, but that situation isn't any more common among warriors than any other segment of the populace—at least I don't believe it is. No, my failures are my own and I'm trying to reconcile them by applying the same dedication I learned as a warrior to the problem at hand.

The absences did, at the time, cause me a great deal of personal distress. I love my children and I hated being away from them. I guess it's good thing that warriorship demands so much—gives you less time to dwell on your own wants and desires.

The cost is justified because the job's important. Indeed, more important than any other because unless the job's done, and done well, everyone in the country could suffer. That includes my family. I did not, however, and would not intentionally sacrifice anyone in my family for the good of the country—myself yes, my family no. I suppose that since I'd had such a splendid life as the son of a warrior, my children would, too. Nonetheless, I would definitely do it again.

WALSH: In human terms the cost has been high. So have the rewards. I have seen things and done things that few people get to experience. It is difficult in the SEAL business just to be competent. I live with men of the same ilk, who want the same things out of life. How does one put a price on this? Does family life suffer? Certainly. If one is married in this business, one must be blessed, as I am, with a woman who stands by you and believes as you do, or at least understands what you're about. In human terms I believe that I am a better man for having lived this life and accepted its challenges. Once this is over, some-day I will have to adjust to the ups and downs of civilian life. That doesn't mean, however, that one must prosti-tute his standards. The same rules apply. "Do the deed." "The only easy day was yesterday."

10. **In many modern conflicts, the warrior is no longer a hero. Often, he is perceived as a villain or a tool of imperialism—if not at home, then in-country or interna-tionally. In some cases, the war he is fighting is on foreign soil, among a divided populace, some of whom consider him a killer, and many of whom may be agents of the enemy in disguise. How does it feel to be an occupying force in a conflict where at least some of the indigenous population hates you as much or more than those you are fighting?**

BARENT: Now I know how the Nazis felt in the countries they invaded.

HARTOV: It is never pleasant to be part of an "occupying" force, unless one is a megalomaniac and enjoys imposing suppression. In Lebanon, I have experienced the full gamut, from being considered a hero of the oppressed to a villain of oppression. A warrior cannot indulge in polit-ical emotionalism and still perform, so we learn to save the philosophizing for leave time.

224

SCHNEIDER: When I believed my cause to be just, I did not worry about those who hated me. When I gave it thought, I tried to do those things that would persuade the occupied people with whom I came in contact that our cause was just.

STEWART: As long as I know what I'm doing is in the best interests of the U.S.A. and that the bulk of American people believe that is so, I feel confident.

WALSH: I've not been in that position, to the best of my knowledge. Vietnam was as close as we have come to being an "occupying force." I don't believe that we ever considered ourselves as occupying that country. What I remember clearly from those days is that we told ourselves over and over again that "We are guests here!"

11. If you could ask the people of the world to change one belief about the combat soldier, what would it be?

HARTOV: That because of the nature of his work, he becomes immune to the suffering of others.

SCHNEIDER: Life should be made possible without combat soldiers. Combat soldiers will eventually turn out to be the sons and daughters of the populace.

STEWART: I don't care about people of the world, just Americans. I think most know what we stand for.

WALSH: Remember that warriors are not supermen. They are human beings with the same feelings and set of values as most of them have. They have simply chosen a different path, less comfortable and closer to the edge. That's where the action is.

Combat

1. What is it like to be in combat?

BARENT: Scary yet exhilarating.

HARTOV: The physical experience is, of course, unique to the individual. It is perhaps akin to standing toes to the edge of a subway platform as an express train rushes by. The cacophony of noise, confusion, adrenaline rush, and attempt to maintain total control expands the senses to a degree that the human body was not intended to duplicate with any regularity.

STEWART: Confused, chaotic. A great challenge that requires calm focus.

SCHNEIDER: I never served in combat in the TV sense. I "cleaned up" after combat immediately after WWII on Okinawa and immediately after the armistice in Korea. I served on MACV staff in Vietnam, I was shot at in the Hue Phu Bay and Tan Son Nhut. The Soviets and East Germans came closer to killing me, however, when they machine-gunned my car, in one incident, and shot out my windows in another.

THOMPSON: Tense.

WALSH: It depends upon what dimension one fights in and what your job is. There are, I believe, different dimensions to combat. For instance, aviators, specifically fighter and attack pilots, as well as the men of the TF 160, are in their own dimension, as are people in submarines and those in the Special Operations Forces (Navy SEALs, Army Special Forces, and Army Rangers). They are unique dimensions of warfare. Then there is the conventional forces dimension. I'm in the unconventional or

Naval Special Forces dimension. The name of the game in Special Operations is to "get in, get it done, and get out." Combat in my dimension is a test of the individual. A special warfare warrior is a team player, but he also knows deep in his gut that individual skills make all the difference. The special warfare warrior, or *operator* as he is known, relies on his personal skill, intelligence, and courage. When I was a young enlisted SEAL going into combat for the first time I *had* to prove myself to myself as well as my peers. I had determined then that were I to die, I should do so as bravely as possible. Sure, I was as scared as anyone else, but I was also *determined* that I would *not* fail. That, as a very young SEAL operator, would have been worse than death. Later as an officer leading a SEAL platoon into combat, I dreaded losing even one man and took great pains to ensure I had all the intelligence and support available. All I could think of was the accomplishment of the mission and getting all my people out of there—alive.

2. **What is the most important thing you learned from your combat experience?**

BARENT: To trust your training and your instincts.

HARTOV: It was a selfish lesson—that I could perform under extreme circumstances.

SCHNEIDER: Have a reason for being where you are.

STEWART: Steady, calm mind and fast action wins.

THOMPSON: That I was less worried about myself than about the mission, and far more afraid of failure than threats to my personal safety.

WALSH: 1. That human life is precious, especially the lives

of my men. The military, no matter what other business it pursues, is in the people business, be it war or peace. If the people don't work properly, nothing else does.

 2. Only the simple succeeds in combat.

 3. War brings out two aspects of human nature: the very best a human being can be and the very worst a human being can be.

3. What is the relationship of comradeship to success in combat?

BARENT: Extremely important.

HARTOV: In my experience, and certainly in the Israel Defense Forces concept, it is everything. We learn to fight as a team, as a single organism, and certainly the more symbiotic the team members, the better the results. Yes, this makes combat death more traumatic for the survivors, but the idea is to win the day.

SCHNEIDER: Comrades help you survive.

STEWART: The cement that glues confidence and overcomes fear.

THOMPSON: Comradeship is all-important to success in combat. The "team" is everything.

WALSH: Be you a simple soldier or a flag officer, unit cohesion is an absolute must to survive. And in the Special Warfare business, it is everything. Like other occupations, the Special Operations business is a personality-driven machine. No question.

4. If you have killed in combat, how did you react the first time? Were your reactions different than what you expected, and if so, how? If you have killed subsequently,

were those experiences different than your initial experience? If so, how were they different?

BARENT: First time—saw it many times in mind's eye. After that, no great reaction—but rarely saw the actual deaths—usually just a big explosion as I killed a truck or a gun.

HARTOV: I have been fortunate in that my killing experiences were never personal, not one-on-one. My unit destroyed a terrorist CP in Lebanon, yet there was no hand-to-hand. We certainly felt justified, with little or no remorse, and we were encouraged to discuss the outcome as a collective. My outfit has a long combat history and we knew what to expect emotionally. Yes, there were some bad dreams and second thoughts, but nothing unanticipated. Since then, we have ambushed a terrorist group again in Lebanon, killing two and capturing one. But again, the effort was collective. When the unit is close knit, each member feels the emotional support that aids in recovery.

SCHNEIDER: To my knowledge I have never killed anyone.

THOMPSON: To my knowledge I've never killed in combat. I've protected others who have, though, and felt nothing more than a sense of disgust that the human condition occasionally made it necessary to do some fairly unpleasant things.

WALSH: The first time I killed a man, he and I were in hand-to-hand combat. It was a moonless night in the Delta region of Vietnam. I was the point man for a SEAL squad and was well ahead of the main body. We had patrolled into a Viet Cong command post deep in enemy territory. The area was considered a Viet Cong

229

stronghold, so much so that the higher ranking enemy officers walked around at night casually without weapons. The enemy officer that I had closed in on tried to kill me with a lethal blow to the left temple. He missed my temple and hit me in the left jawbone, almost knocking me unconscious and knocking my weapon (AK-47) from my hand. I was dressed in a Viet Cong uniform and he originally mistook me for one of his own guards, which was how I was able to get that close in the first place. After knocking me down he turned to look for my weapon. We scrambled for it and I got to it first. At that point he turned to flee and I fired. I fired seven times, hitting him six. I remember standing there with my mouth open for a few seconds looking at what I just done. He didn't even look like the same man I had just been fighting with. It was the first time in my life that I observed death in someone's eyes and knew, without being told, what it was. And I will never forget the smell of combat. It is cordite mixed with blood mixed with sweat mixed with fear mixed with adrenaline, and you can smell the energy in the air, and sometimes taste the bile forming in your stomach, when death is very close, and you've made it through—again. I remember feeling very much alive after the above and many similar incidents afterward.

During subsequent encounters the process became more mechanical. Gone was the novelty and the excitement. Now it was business. I began to think more about the whole process. I would rehearse what I would do in this or that situation. I figured that if I kept conditioning my mind that I could expect myself to react appropriately when necessary. My senses began to develop unbelievably. We learned how to become invisible in the jungle.

Those who have practiced, know. We would hide off a known enemy commo-liaison route and watch patrols go by. At times they were so close I would close my eyes so the whites wouldn't show. The focus of effort in being invisible during those times was to observe from the periphery of your eyes and not concentrate your attention on the target. People's baser animal instincts become truly alive in combat, not only ours, but theirs as well. It's a two-way street. There were times when someone in our squad could feel something up ahead or something that was about to happen. More than once we were able to avoid being ambushed ourselves by the hair standing up on the back of someone's neck. Lots to be said for instinct in the jungle, or wherever else you find yourself.

5. How does it feel to see a comrade die in combat? What do you tell yourself when you survive and your friends don't?

BARENT: How lucky I am.

HARTOV: When a comrade dies in action, you experience a range of emotions from survivor relief to a sense of remorse and even guilt. However, as all warriors are acutely aware of the risks, one becomes somewhat fatalistic, realizing that the unfortunate results are often simply an issue of mathematics.

SCHNEIDER: I never saw a military comrade die in combat. I saw my wife die by my side because of a moment's inattention on my part. I will never forget.

STEWART: Every dead soldier is a brother. It is sad, final, tragic. You move on to new periods in your life.

THOMPSON: One of the factors I've personally come to grips with is the fact of my own mortality—everyone

231

dies—even me. And it's just a matter of where or when. So, I'm very fatalistic about the whole thing. When your time's up, it's up.

In addition to the inevitability of physical death, I also believe "death" is either everlasting peace or everlasting "life." So, I can't say that I feel especially sorry for the friends I've lost. I do, however, feel an enormous sense of personal loss. I grieve not only for myself but for everyone else left behind, especially the relatives of my friends and for the world in general. These men had much, much to offer.

As an aside, death has struck very close to me. Briefly, my crew and I were returning to the USS *Independence* following a routine EA6B mission south of Cyprus: nice day, light seas. We flew a good pattern to an OK pass and engaged the carriers' number three wire.

At first the arrested landing appeared to be normal. However, within a second after touchdown, the normal deceleration experienced during an arrested landing ceased. Although we didn't know exactly what was wrong, we did know that the aircraft was in jeopardy and all three of us initiated ejection. Each of the ejections were successful, with the only difference being that I and one other of the crew released our parachutes before we entered the water. The last crew member, the thirty-one-year-old pilot, did not. He landed in the water immediately in front of the crashed aircraft and his chute draped itself across the nose of the plane. He apparently was also entangled in the chute, because when the plane sank, it pulled him under with it. His body was never recovered.

The other crew member and I were picked up by SAR helicopters and returned to the ship. Neither of us was injured. Investigation revealed that the tail hook "stinger" or hooktip had forced itself between the strands of the arresting gear cable. Therefore, only two of the six strands of the cable were actually engaged. These two strands parted under the force of the arrested landing. Unfortunately, by that time the aircraft was too slow to fly, but still too fast to stop. If fell off the edge of the ship.

WALSH: When a close teammate dies on you, it is important to acknowledge the death and accept it. It happened. It is also important not to dwell on it too much and continue to operate. It also simply means that it is time to go. In that respect, we are all in the same boat.

The World

1. **Why do you think major world powers such as the United States and U.S.S.R. fare so badly against Third World countries such as Vietnam and Afghanistan?**

BARENT: We don't know and respect their beliefs.

HARTOV: Technology is no match for a man with a mission who believes he is righteous. A large army can defeat small indigenous forces, but that army's commanders must be brilliant, innovative, and prepared to rapidly adjust. These are not traits common to high-ranking military bureaucrats.

SCHNEIDER: They are not defending their homeland and the opponents are.

STEWART: Goals unclear. Messianic belief that we can "do it for them."

THOMPSON: These wars failed because there was no widespread popular support within either Vietnam or Afghanistan, nor within the U.S. and USSR for that matter. The U.S. is making the same mistake in Central America in general and El Salvador in particular. We'll never "win" there either.

WALSH: Both the U.S. and the Soviets failed to realize that the folks we were fighting were very determined people who knew what they were fighting for. What were we fighting for?

2. **To what do you credit U.S. successes in Grenada, Panama, and Iraq? If you feel these actions have been less than successful, tell why.**

BARENT: Good leadership in Iraq. The others weren't quite as good.

HARTOV: In the matters of Grenada and Panama, the U.S. efforts were technically successful, although the objectives were attained by virtue of shear quantitative advantage. However, as learning experiences these "incidents" were invaluable. In the matter of the Gulf War, we witnessed a rarity in military history—an entire military and political complex learning a historical lesson (from the quagmire of Vietnam) and applying those lessons in a brilliant application of tactical force. Operation Desert Storm was a military success precisely because President Bush kept his objective at the forefront and his troops, from Chief of Staff to privates in the field, knew that they were fully supported both logistically and emotionally. However, Saddam Hussein still lives, which is in my opinion a primary objective left unresolved.

SCHNEIDER: Overwhelming power, reasonably rapidly applied.

STEWART: Clear goals, supported by American people. Objectives matched our will and ability to accomplish them.

WALSH: We had wise political leadership in that the Commander-in-Chief acted decisively, the military delivered as ordered and Congress watched it on TV and stayed out of the way. Things were looking up.

3. If you had the chance to change one thing your government has done during your service, what would it be?

BARENT: To have removed the restrictions in Vietnam. To do in '65–'66 what Goldwater propounded and Nixon actually did in '72.

HARTOV: I would not have allowed the government to vacillate in its policy of handling the uprisings in the territories (the "West Bank" and Gaza). The lack of direction put an impossible burden on our young troops, destroying morale and denuding the concept of "A Purity Of Arms." A government has an obligation to its young warriors, like a parent to its children. If that parent is unguided, what can it expect of its offspring?

SCHNEIDER: I would have commanded the 525 MI Group in Vietnam.

STEWART: State clear goals for our involvement in Vietnam and mobilize the reserves during the period.

THOMPSON: I'd depoliticize the military and fire every civil servant in DOD about the grade of GS-7.

WALSH: 1. I would change the way in which our government conducted the Vietnam War. Or should I say *failed* to conduct the war. 'Nuff said there.

2. At the risk of sounding unprofessional, I still to this day believe that Jane Fonda knowingly and without remorse betrayed her country. If we had it to do over again, I'd have changed the law to prohibit such activities, especially with troops in the field, and hopefully, after a fair trial, witnessed her execution. In this belief I am not alone.

4. Some nations still draft soldiers; some do not. How do you think conscription affects a fighting force?

BARENT: I used to think it helped—now not sure. But it definitely helps civilians because teachers, preachers, intellectuals, wealthy, etc., would all have to serve and that would enrich our people and broaden their outlook.

HARTOV: This depends entirely on the nation and its culture. In Israel, conscription is viewed as a fact of life, and rejection from conscription can be considered a great dishonor. In that country, the military mirrors society in beneficial ways, giving the armed forces a universal pool of talent which it requires. However, in the United States conscription is viewed differently depending on the circumstances. During WWII it was considered a duty and honor. During Vietnam, the relative ease with which the draft could be avoided gave the military a negative balance and fostered resentment. On the other hand, Desert Storm was fought with only professional soldiers, and we witnessed an incredible rise in the will and ability to fight.

SCHNEIDER: Conscripted troops fight just as well as volunteers, if they know why they are there.

STEWART: It can degrade it through low morale. On the other hand, it offers the populace as a whole a wholesome, shared experience of service.

THOMPSON: If the people within a society feel a sense of responsibility to the society, then conscription will be viewed as a necessary price to pay for the security of the society. In these instances, conscription is a positive, indeed essential and effective factor in the overall defensive posture of the nation. Israel, Germany, and Switzerland rather exemplify this conclusion. If, on the other hand, the general society is too "individual" oriented, such as it is in the United States, conscription is really more trouble than it's worth.

WALSH: If I had my way, everyone would serve. All males would put their time in. There would be no excuses. Time was when most men in this country did some time in the military. It gave us more of a common bond with each other, and there were a lot fewer wimps running around. The time spent in the military gave many a young man a chance to grow up, to see what he was made of, a little of his world, and helped many a young man decide what direction he wanted to go in life. While I am a believer in the all-volunteer force, and also believe that today's military is the best ever, I still believe that we should have conscription of all males. Those truly unqualified should be required to serve for two years in some other public service. Our country would prosper from this.

5. **Today's missions are often run with real command in the hands of the highest levels of authority back home, no matter how far away the action is and what commanders on the ground would prefer. How can we streamline command decision making and adapt to this process? to other results of high-tech warfighting technology?**

237

BARENT: Do like Bush and Powell: Don't talk or ask questions (just the opposite of Carter).

HARTOV: This trend is an unfortunate result of technology superseding common sense. Despite the ability to direct from a standoff position, we should only adjust in terms of using our increased access to real-time intelligence. The relationship of high-ranking commander to field general should be no different than that of a battalion C.O. to his captain. Give the man his mission, supply him with intelligence and logistical support, then hands off and let him run. If you don't trust him, replace him.

SCHNEIDER: Technology can be applied to speeding up decisions. The literature abounds.

STEWART: The President will always be the final arbiter. That's our system. He weighs political, economic, and military aspects. Technology won't change that. It shouldn't.

THOMPSON: Don't even try—command of forces by anyone other than the commander on the scene is doomed to failure. Military force should be the last resort of any nation in its dealings with other nations. However, once military force is committed, leave the battle to the professionals at the scene of the action.

WALSH: Minds greater and wiser than mine are working that problem at the highest levels. Stay tuned.

6. **How do you feel about the micro-management of war-fighting by civilian authorities? Did the events of Desert Shield/Storm change how you feel about the relationship to the legislative and executive branches?**

BARENT: 1. It will kill you. 2. No, because Bush did not make the mistakes LBJ and McNamara did.

HARTOV: A leading question, but I'll bite. Civilians may have to legislate the overall directive, but then they should withdraw completely. The incredibly moronic arguments put forth by U.S. legislators in favor of desisting from action in the Gulf nearly stayed the President's hand. These were the most disturbing moments of the conflict.

SCHNEIDER: Micro-management stifles initiative, no matter where it takes place. In most instances that is bad. If your middle managers are not capable or trustworthy, micro-management may be the only way. The Soviet echelon-ning system was a reasonable response to a situation in which the junior leaders were neither capable nor reliable. The relationship between the branches of government was well established by the Constitution. It should be left alone. It is not broken.

STEWART: Vietnam was a disaster of micro-management, largely because political leaders did not establish clear and clearly supported national goals. Desert Shield/Storm objectives were clearly stated, fully supported. Mission orders sufficed because national leaders established stra-tegic parameters. An unqualified success.

THOMPSON: Allowing civilian authorities to micro-manage military operations is like allowing the next of kin to supervise open heart surgery, only worse. At least the next of kin has something to lose if the surgery fails. This probably accounts for the reluctance of the next of kin to interfere with the surgeon except to authorize the surgery in the first place. Civilian authorities, unfortunately, do not feel similarly restrained.

Every military failure suffered by American armed forces is the direct result of micro-management by civilian authorities. These include Vietnam, the Iranian hostage rescue attempt, the occupation of Beirut airport, and the 1983 strike on Syrian positions near Beirut.

The 1983 strike against the Syrians, which I flew, exemplifies the result of civilian micro-management, which is to say, disaster. In this mission, the TOT (Time On Target), as dictated by civilian authorities, did not allow enough time to properly prepare for the mission. Civilian authorities also changed the targets we'd been planning to strike for months. This, in turn, required additional planning as well as changing ordnance loads, neither of which could be accomplished in the time available. Requests by the Battle Group commander, RADM Jetty O. Tuttle, to delay the mission were ignored by the civilian authorities, as well as by the military chain of command.

Why was it so important to hit the Syrians at the time specified? It was because our civilian authorities wanted to have a successful mission reported in time to make the morning edition of the *Washington Post*. This attempt to make news cost one American dead, one captured, one who had to be rescued, two American planes destroyed and one other damaged, not to mention the Syrians who may have been killed or injured and the Lebanese civilians hurt and killed when one of our damaged airplanes crashed in a residential section of Beirut.

The problem with civilian authorities is that they act on a different set of motives than military people do, and these motives are often suspect. Let's face it, even if the Syrian strikes had gone well, one must necessarily ask whether anyone's life, even a Syrian soldier's, was worth a little newsprint.

Concurrently, there can be no debate with respect to "control" of the warfighting by civilian authorities. In a democracy, there simply isn't any other option. However, this control should be exercised only by elected civilian authorities and extend only to the decision to go to war.

Desert Shield and Desert Storm may end up as textbook examples of how civilian control of warfighting should be effected. That is, civilian authorities took the decision to commit forces, but the operation itself was left in the hands of the professionals. Other operations executed under the same general circumstances include virtually every conflict America has been engaged in until Vietnam, as well as Grenada (1983), all operations near Libya (1981–1987), and the Panamanian operation. Simply stated, every successful military operation undertaken by the American armed forces has been characterized by the general absence of micro-management by civilian authorities.

Desert Shield and Desert Storm may also be used to exemplify the relationship of the executive and legislative branches with respect to warfighting. These branches of government are adversarial by design and can, therefore, be expected to react accordingly. But the President was also designated Commander-in-Chief by design, and his authority to commit troops in a limited conflict is implicit, not to mention necessary in a military sense—for example, in achieving a element of surprise. He should, however, seek congressional approval when time allows.

Warfighting simply cannot be handled by committee, especially legislative committee. The awful truth is that the legislature is the weakest, least capable, most corrupt, least intelligent, and least informed of the three branches.

To allow these people to influence military operations, beyond that very limited degree explicit in the Constitution, is the height of folly.

In the final analysis, then, we have to put up with the elected civilian authorities because that's the way it has to be in a democracy. But I personally draw the line at appointed authorities. I've always resented the fact that my oath of office required that I follow the orders of the Secretary of Defense and the Secretary of the Navy. These men are not elected, they are appointed and are, therefore, just as likely to be your standard, shallow, self-serving political hack as anything else. And, I absolutely refuse to acknowledge the authority of career civilian servants. If these fellows want to give orders, they can put on the suit.

WALSH: Things are getting better. Confidence in the military has never been higher.

7. **Is America in decline militarily or are we truly the one remaining superpower, capable of leading the world into a new century?**

BARENT: Not on decline.

HARTOV: One does not lead the world into a new century by military might. We do so by concentrating on educating our children. A superpower is only so if its moral fabric equals its muscular flex.

SCHNEIDER: If we don't restore the family, we will not be capable of anything.

STEWART: Militarily, we're a superpower. Our underlying economic and educational structures and national identity (through shared clear values) are at risk.

THOMPSON: From a purely military point of view, we're doing pretty well on the conventional battlefield and I don't think any drastic changes are in order. If by "unconventional" you mean Special Operations, I'd like to see more direct military control, for example, CIA control with the caveat that military officers take these operations more seriously. If, on the other hand, you equate unconventional warfare to nuclear warfare (which is usually the case), then I think we're doing the best we can now.

WALSH: We are surely capable. Whether or not we remain capable is unfortunately in the hands of many entities that are not elected, such as the Council on Foreign Relations. Admittedly we have no choice in this day and age except to be a very international superpower. However, recall George Washington's admonition to beware of becoming involved in "foreign entanglements." Wonder what old George would say if he could see us now?

8. How does the press affect military operations today?

BARENT: Zip because DAO knows what to do.

HARTOV: Unfortunately, the press has become an unobjective morass of glory-seeking hounds whose objective is to create profit-making sensations rather than to observe and report. Even more unfortunate, our politicians tend to make their decisions based upon the projected media response rather than on the potential benefits of a given action. At least in America, military operations rapidly become media circuses. The results are almost always negative, in that commanders feel compelled to explain themselves.

SCHNEIDER: The press/media have made military operations more hazardous.

STEWART: Affects the political level, which in turn pressures military. Also makes military decision makers and planners wary of media. Cannot trust them to hold back even when soldiers are in jeopardy.

THOMPSON: Generally negative. Reporters are right up there in the running with politicians where self-serving behavior is concerned. I will say that the average politician is probably smarter and better informed than the average reporter, though. To coin a phrase, reporters are basically stupid, but some are sly and cunning and bear watching.

WALSH: While I am a firm believer in First Amendment rights, the press, in my judgment, very often ignores the concept of Operations Security (OPSEC) that military operations must have.

9. **A Washington think tank recently did a survey suggesting that the results of televised violence on civilian populations has been to make those populations more ready to accept repression if it promises security. Do you agree? Why? If not, what effect do you think the media has on the way the warrior is perceived by noncombatants?**

BARENT: Two different questions. 1. Yes. 2. Up to a year or so ago it made us look bad.

HARTOV: A liberal female friend recently remarked to me that she is prepared to have martial law imposed in New York City. This is not the first such talk I have heard, so I must conclude that the think tank's conclusions are correct.

SCHNEIDER: I agree that televised and media-spread views of violence have conditioned populaces to accept repression because they show violence as the result of freedom, not loss of values.

STEWART: Do not agree, but believe the media presents two unrealistic aspects of war—that it is "bloodless" and that officers are inept or mentally inflexible.

THOMPSON: I agree with the survey. Throughout history, people have been willing to trade freedom for security, at least for finite periods of time. Indeed, never a day goes by when some faction or another of our society isn't demanding that "the government" make some other faction of society do something it doesn't want to do. The result is repression. In any event, the only part the media plays in the equation is that its reporting tends to aggravate popular insecurity and therefore renders them ever more prepared to accept the repression for which government in general is characterized.

WALSH: Yes. I believe that people are, or should be, responsible for their own security. We as a nation have come to reply too much on the police for (so-called) protection. The media continues to hammer away at masculinity by portraying masculinity as Rambo-ish, or the man of the house as an incompetent boob. Rubbish.

10. **Do you believe that an international strike force can and should be created to counter terrorists, despots, and narcotics czars? If so, how would you structure such a force?**

BARENT: Yes—in great secrecy.

HARTOV: The interests of nations change like the weather, and therefore international strike forces are always at risk of dilution due to political changes, not to mention penetration. I do not see this as a realistic or effective solution. Works great in comic books.

SCHNEIDER: No, do not try to construct an offensive inter-national force.

STEWART: No. I don't believe the U.S. should trust its interests to others, especially where violent action might be necessary.

THOMPSON: Yes. I think such a strike force would be created and structured along the lines we've already witnessed in Desert Shield and Desert Storm. However, if the degree of cooperation required to create such a strike force actually comes to pass, it is reasonable to assume that many of the problems dictating the need for the strike force will be handled internally.

WALSH: I would prefer not to comment at this time.

11. It is said that an occupying force can seldom defeat a hostile indigenous populace. Is this proposition true, and how does it affect the missions we will be facing as the world's power blocs realign?

BARENT: Don't go where the public really doesn't want us to.

HARTOV: The premise is true. A force can seldom defeat a hostile indigenous population, but by definition this ob-jective is a mistake. An imposing force should attempt to "buy" the population, not defeat it. But this is the role of sophisticated policy managers, of which there are few of any great talent.

SCHNEIDER: It is a matter of degree. The Soviet Communist army defeated the Soviet people for sixty years.

STEWART: We shouldn't be occupying a hostile land.

THOMPSON: Of course, a hostile indigenous populace can be defeated—if you care to create an occupying force that exceeds the sum total of the number of people in the populace. A penchant for mercilessness is also helpful. Check the books, there has never been a successful occupation of any kind, let alone one where the populace was totally hostile.

WALSH: No. Look at what the British did in Malaysia after WWII. Incidentally, the Brits are still the only ones to do a truly successful counterinsurgency campaign. Those lessons are still very valid.

12. Describe the misconceptions that civilians have of the warrior class. Do these misconceptions affect you? If so, how?

BARENT: 1. Evil killers. 2. Not much, because I don't care what they think. Fighter pilots rarely respond to public opinion.

HARTOV: Civilians, of course, tend to think that all warriors live for the next fight, that they are social anomalies. U.S. civilians do not understand me, but I require only respect, not understanding. On the other hand, in Israel there is no such thing as a pure "civilian," so this conflict does not exist.

SCHNEIDER: Warriors are ill-educated brutes who love to kill—Conan the Barbarian types. They are waiting to take over the government at the slightest whim. I worry that someone might believe that to be true. I do my best to disabuse society of the stereotype.

STEWART: Believe Generals Powell and Schwartzkopf cleared up the misconception that military people are narrow minded, lack intelligence, and feel little compassion.

THOMPSON: Perhaps the greatest misconception is that soldiers and sailors are so steeped in military discipline that they can do nothing but follow orders. This, of course, is incorrect. In actuality, every soldier and sailor is trained to lead, and before he or she can lead, he or she must be able to think clearly and act quickly. Therefore, the average military person is far more decisive and far more able to exert a positive influence on those around him than the average civilian. Oddly enough, decisiveness is not a trait that is in particular demand in our society, and leadership, of the variety practiced in the military, is a totally alien concept.

The negative effects of civilian misconceptions materialize even for active-duty service people. For example, pay is usually based on the soldier's "equivalent" civilian occupation. The fact is that a soldier has no equivalent civilian occupation. Imagine how much it would cost to pay Navy men and women rated merchant seaman equal pay and stipulate that these people work only six months a year.

WALSH: I'm convinced that people in general watch too much TV. The civilian population as a whole is quite uninformed as to the *Ethos* a true warrior must possess to do his job. The effect it all has on me is that I have been answering the same questions for twenty-five years.

The Future

1. **What do you see as the single greatest threat to security in the coming decade? In the coming century?**

BARENT: U.S. apathy and complacency.

HARTOV: Global technological capabilities are proliferating as social moral structures are deteriorating. This means that more lethal weapons of destruction will become more accessible to smaller radical factions of political and narco-terrorists. If trends continue, one could envision a mid-21st century where Los Angeles drug gangs possess hand-held particle beam "destructors." I hope that I am exaggerating.

SCHNEIDER: Decay of family values both in the decade and the coming century.

STEWART: The deterioration of U.S. values and education.

THOMPSON: External threats will be underdeveloped, but well-armed Third World nations and the dictatorial leaders that go with them will need to be watched. Our most serious threat is internal in that we seem to have lost our sense of direction.

WALSH: I believe that the greatest single threat to the United States is that we will negate our leadership of the free world, by allowing non-elected entities, such as the Council on Foreign Relations, to weaken our national sovereignty. I believe that they and others of their ilk will eventually cause the United States to give in to the *World Government* concept before the American people really catch on to just how much they could forfeit in terms of their individual freedoms. In my view we have already begun to tread down that path. Witness how much we, as a nation, made damn sure that we had the blessings of the UN before so much as twitching a muscle in Desert Storm. We are supposed to be a superpower, a world leader. A leader takes risks.

2. **If you had to guess at the map of world powers in ten years, where would the flash points be? in twenty years?**

BARENT: 10 years—Japan, South America, Russia, Balkans. 20 years—Africa, Japan, Russia, South America.

HARTOV: Only a fool would try to answer the question, with my apologies to those who made a polite guess.

SCHNEIDER: A.D.2000: Middle East; Central America. A.D.2010: Southeast Asia; South America—Heroin Country.

STEWART: 10 years—Middle East. 20 years—Middle East, South Asia.

THOMPSON: Central and South America are always good bets, as is Africa and the Middle East. Oddly enough, I also believe that we will see a good bit of flashing here in the United States as we are no longer distracted by the threat from the "Evil Empire" and have to deal with our own social, economic, and political problems.

WALSH: The Middle East, Latin America, and the Pacific Rim.

3. **Do you see religious or sect fundamentalism as an evolving threat in the Third World? Do you think different tactics are necessary to fight a fundamentalist army? If so, what kind?**

BARENT: 1. Definite yes. 2. Probably—if they go human wave on their way to "heaven."

HARTOV: Religious and sect fundamentalism is definitely a *continuing* and increasing threat in the Third World. Unfortunately, when fighting a fundamentalist army one must assume a degree of cruelty nearly equal to the enemy's, for the extreme use of force is the only thing that can deter him, and the only thing he understands.

SCHNEIDER: Fundamentalism is a clear threat to stability. A fundamentalist army may execute orders without regard to human life; that possibility must be considered in planning for military operations.

STEWART: The U.S. should stay out of religious wars.

THOMPSON: Religious and sect fundamentalism as an evolving threat here in the United States. "True believers" are always dangerous no matter who or where they are because they don't feel that they have to answer to anyone but whichever deity or religion they follow. Therefore, any sort of behavior on their part is justified.

Different tactics, per se, aren't really required. But the defeat of these types of forces must be overwhelming and utterly decisive. Bluntly, many more will need to be killed or seriously wounded than would be the case were the battle more "civilized."

Psychological warfare, if properly carried out, should be especially effective against these armies. Defeat the belief, or even install a reason to doubt the belief, and you've defeated the soldier or at least degraded his will to fight.

WALSH: Yes. We don't necessarily need different tactics. We already know what we are doing. The question is, how well will we do it? The military will act on the will of its civilian leadership. Bottom line.

4. **Many analysts believe that low-intensity conflict, counterterrorism, counterinsurgency, and counternarcotics will be the threats we must combat in the coming century. If you agree, how would you suggest we improve our performance in these areas? If you disagree, say what threats you see as most compelling.**

BARENT: Agree. Kill, don't capture.

HARTOV: I agree with the analysts. As I stated above, I would concentrate on educating our warriors in the areas of concern, rather than simply honing our fighting skills. "Know thine enemy."

SCHNEIDER: I agree—read Bernard Fall again.

STEWART: Mid-intensity conflict is more likely due to pro-liferation of weapon's technology.

WALSH: The threats iterated above all are external threats. We will deal with that. The internal threats are equally important. I am the furthest thing alive from a liberal. However, as I grow more into the role of aging warrior I am concerned with the chipping away of our basic Con-stitutional rights and the ease with which the American people are giving them up. Scary.

5. **No matter how the superpowers and democratic societies strive for peace, emerging Third World nations will re-quire the developed nations to maintain a state of readi-ness in the future. What sort of readiness is required in a future where, although the term "warfighting" may be replaced by "peacekeeping," conflicts will still occur and men of many nations will still die in those conflicts?**

BARENT: High readiness but not as large a force as when war with Russia was a possibility.

HARTOV: As previously stated, I believe that desperation will force some factions to adapt desperate measures. "Peacekeeping" forces will not only be required to main-tain high degrees of readiness to defeat nuclear, chemical, and biological threats, but those forces must be ready and willing to *preempt*. This requires great amounts of con-

viction, will, and fortitude, without fear of political ram-
ifications.

STEWART: Force projection, readiness. Synchronized operations in joint *and* combined commands.

WALSH: The Special Operations Forces live by keeping their
rucksacks ready to go anyway. They just need to know
where to go. Also, my experience in Lebanon and Latin
America has taught me that there is no such thing as
"peacekeeping." I hope and pray that we never get into
another situation like Lebanon again. That wasn't
peacekeeping—that was lunacy. As for the future, no
change, keep your rucksack ready to go.

6. **We are entering a period of massive reduction in force and
restructuring of the world's armed forces. If you could
advise the world's policy makers, how would you guide
this process to maintain and improve readiness and strike
capability while reducing the size of today's forces?**

BARENT: Go for quality troops and leaders.

HARTOV: In the military, as in the corporate world, simple
reduction of forces is self-defeating if it is not selective.
One must retain the most talented individuals, pay them
well, motivate and educate them. The world's elite forces
have proved time and again that "less is more" when the
blade is short but the cutting edge sharp.

SCHNEIDER: The United States and "West" or "North"
must sacrifice its comfort for its long-term survival.
Within that framework we should maintain adequate
force to impose a Pax Americana.

STEWART: Go slow—over 10 years—address a clear national
strategy and seek public approval for it. Improve strategic
deployability.

THOMPSON: My advice to world policy makers would be to create the degree of stability inside and outside their countries to a point where military spending could be done away with altogether. Barring that, I'd urge them to create the finest defensive forces possible, using the Swiss as their model.

WALSH: We may not have six months to get ready next time a contingency like Desert Storm/Desert Shield arises. We need to work on our sea and air lift capability.

7. **What improvements would you like to make in the way force is projected on the conventional battlefield? on the unconventional battlefield?**

BARENT: Can't say.

HARTOV: On the conventional battlefield, I would like to see further emphasis on real-time tactical intelligence, by further use of drones, robotics, and deep penetration human gathering. Conventional forces should respond to developing battlefield needs rather than advancing in set-piece predetermined moves. On the unconventional battlefield, we must always bring the fight to the enemy and never remain in static emplacements. Less force, more aptly applied, is always the rule in unconventional circumstances.

SCHNEIDER: Make optimum use of technology to "get thar fustest with the mostest." Any battlefield.

STEWART: Conventionally—better intel capability with smart weapons. Unconventionally, only get involved where absolutely necessary for direct U.S. interests. Do so with a package of political, economic, social, *and* (lastly) military measures.

WALSH: I can only address the unconventional battlefield. The National Command Authority must consider even more carefully the timely application of Special Operations Forces well ahead of conflict. When it comes right down to it, it then becomes a political decision. The moment you deploy Special Operations Forces, you have declared war. In the political realm, where the real decisions are made, timing is everything. I would also like to see the conventional commanders make it more obvious to the Special Operations Forces what their objectives are. SOFs very existence is to support the conventional effort. It helps to know what the objectives of a particular war plan are ahead of time to "train the force."

8. **What have we learned about low-intensity and regional conflict while fighting in the Third World that should change the way we approach such combat in the future?**

BARENT: Don't know.

HARTOV: That the "Third World," as referred to here, is not a single entity or arena and should not be considered as such. Each conflict is different, each population's concept of warfare is indigenous to its own culture. A professional warrior should never assume that what worked in the last arena will work once again in the next.

SCHNEIDER: Make sure we know why we are there, and communicate that to the troops.

STEWART: Focus national objectives on what's best for U.S. interests and where possible act in concert with an international coalition. In LIC [Low-Intensity Conflict], required the host nation to take the lead or don't get involved.

THOMPSON: First, there's no such thing as "low-intensity" conflict and to view any conflict as "low-intensity" is the first step to defeat. I think we've already learned how to approach these conflicts, which is to say, with overwhelming, fast-moving force against clearly defined military objectives.

9. **How can we use what we've learned from urban combat, jungle and desert warfare to best advantage as our larger forces become more like the "special forces" of the late twentieth century?**

BARENT: Don't lose the ability.

HARTOV: The military complex tends to promote innovation while shunting aside the experience of the "old soldier." We must retain those veterans of jungle and desert warfare, nurture them and place them in positions to pass on their legacies to the next generation of warriors. Even larger forces should pass through Special Warfare centers, where the details of unconventional warfighting can be absorbed.

SCHNEIDER: Be careful not to draw the wrong lessons, ignoring other possibilities.

STEWART: Don't understand the question.

WALSH: Train the force, equip the force, and take care of the force.

10. **What do you believe the warrior of the future will face as the greatest threat to personal survival?**

BARENT: Some REMF wanting shinier shoes or cleaner tank treads or prettier aircraft or painted rocks.

HARTOV: We witnessed a hint of things to come in the

recent Gulf War, even though it did not come to pass. The warrior of the future will face some very nasty chemical and biological enemies on the battlefield.

SCHNEIDER: Loss of family values.

STEWART: Attacks from smart weapons, deeply delivered.

WALSH: Electronic warfare and laser threats.

11. **The warrior of the future will be a techno-commando, complete with magic black boxes and satellite uplinks at his command. Describe the warrior of the future, including the dream A-Team and equipment package of your choice.**

BARENT: As a fighter pilot, I'll leave this one to the A-Team to decide.

HARTOV: My warrior of the future has a Ph.D. in linguistics and political science, plus a black belt in one of the traditional martial arts. Aside from that, the rest is just hardware.

SCHNEIDER: I am sure someone with experience can do a better job here.

STEWART: This is "Star Trek" stuff, the kind that make the American people have great misconceptions, unrealistic expectations.

WALSH: The dream A-Team, as you call it, exists today. The average SOF (Army, Navy, AF) guy must still rely on his personal skill, intelligence, and courage. Those basic tenets will remain unchanged, no matter how technologically advanced this business becomes. All the technical devices do is make the job easier, be it communications or laser target designation. And lest we forget, it is our enlisted people who are the true skill in the Special Warfare business. That fact will also remain unchanged.

12. **Do you think women will play a greater combat role in warfare in the future? In Canada, Israel, and other nations, women are assuming greater combat responsibilities. The United States is slowly—and reluctantly—testing women in the field. How would you feel—or how have you felt—when fighting with women on your team or under your command?**

BARENT: Can't say.

HARTOV: Correction—women in Israel are assuming greater combat *training* roles, but we have always tried to extract them from actual engagements. We do not have female fighter pilots, tankers or infantry, except in training or support roles. The United States is making great strides in incorporating women into combat roles, and I respect but do not envy those women. Woman are deservedly attaining equality in all forms of U.S. life, from the workplace to the military. However, the ability and necessity to kill is not necessarily an admirable goal. I would not like to have women on my combat team—not because they might not perform the tasks, but precisely because it would sadden me to see them kill and be killed.

SCHNEIDER: Women were never under my command in combat. I believe women do not belong on the field of combat. I believe women can perform all the other functions of an armed force as well as men. If you made pregnancy cause for instant dismissal from the service, without prejudice or medical benefit beyond the delivery, you might make allowing women in combat barely tolerable in the armed forces.

STEWART: Women are capable. Set equal standards, not double standards.

THOMPSON: In theory, I see no reason why women shouldn't play a greater combat role in future warfare. I don't even see why the services can't make at least minimal changes to accommodate women. I do not, however, see the advancement of women in the military as a quest or crusade that must be pursued at all costs.

Theory aside, it's been my experience that women, while very proficient under normal conditions, don't adjust very well to the hardships of military life. Thus they become a burden to the command rather than an asset. When this happens, the lady simply has to go. I would point out that there are also men who become more of a burden than an asset, and the same rules apply. Ironically, most officers are willing to give the women more latitude than they will the men. This also isn't so good.

WALSH: I hope not. Proverbs 31:3 warns men not to give their strength to women. The word *strength* in this context means military might. I believe that an all-male draft is the answer. That way we won't have to find out the hard way that Solomon was right after all. I'm not convinced that the Canadians or the Israelis are using their females to the extent that the liberal press wants us to believe. There are enough men in this country to do the job. If we reinstate conscription for all, with no excuses for anyone, we'll have enough to do the job. We'll also have a manpower pool of sufficiently trained men to recall when we need to. And before you label me anything, I am happily married to a Navy lieutenant in the Nurse Corps. I have no reservation about women in the military. I have reservations about women in combat roles. No military should have more than 4 to 5 percent female.

13. **What is the role of special forces and unconventional warriors in the armies of the future? What will the armies of the future be like?**

HARTOV: Due to the increasing love affair with technology, I predict greater usage of robotics, until perhaps even armored columns are unmanned and directed by "desk warriors." However, special forces will take on even more significance and possibly become the primary manpower elements. All of the Allied Coalition smart bombs put together could not eliminate Saddam Hussein—this could have, and *should have* been executed by the use of special forces. Their importance will not diminish.

SCHNEIDER: Guerilla warfare must be fought with guerilla warfare, counternarcotics and counterterrorism the same. There should be a full spectrum of force from low-intensity conflict to high-intensity. The bad guys will up the ante to that stage whether the good guys do or not.

STEWART: CT, training host nations, hostage rescue, force projection. Modern armies will be lighter, more firepower and accuracy, better ability to see the environment and quickly decide accurately.

WALSH: Eventually I believe that SOF will be used as an instrument of national will across the full spectrum of conflict. The nation's confidence in its Special Operations Forces is continuing to grow. I am personally grateful for the Goldwater-Nichols Act. It is the best thing that ever happened to this business. In the next five years we will have truly matured professionally and will go on from there.

14. **What is the place of quick-reaction forces in the warfare of the future?**

BARENT: Very important.

HARTOV: On Point.

SCHNEIDER: They are the Alpha and Omega.

STEWART: Power projection, support policy, deterrence.

THOMPSON: Quick-reaction forces play the same role in future warfare as they do today, i.e., on the cutting edge. The major difference is that, with luck, these "shock troops" will apply enough shock to solve the problem rather than merely hold the fort until "regular" forces arrive. As an aside, the quick-reaction concept isn't new. Indeed, the Navy/Marine team have always represented a quick-reaction capability. Airborne forces can also react quickly, but in a limited sort of way, because airplanes only carry so much equipment.

WALSH: Keep your rucksack ready to go.

15. What is the place of human intelligence collection in the future?

BARENT: Vital

HARTOV: It cannot be overemphasized. Although we have come to rely on some very sophisticated technological intelligence devices, there is no substitute for having an agent in the enemy camp.

SCHNEIDER: There will always be a requirement to find out the innermost secrets of the opposing force. That can still only be done by HUMINT.

STEWART: Warning, reveal political and military intent, will on the part of political and military leaders.

WALSH: We're way behind the power curve. We seem to keep relearning the painful lesson of overreliance on high-technology. Human intelligence gathering is not

261

the glamour job it is portrayed as. Also, it takes years to get that kind of effort going to where a solid data base is built. I would hope that if a national decision is made in this regard, that the director of Central Intelligence will be legally empowered by Congress to be the HUMINT czar and properly manage the national effort. In this way we would better manage the collection effort, set priorities, and (hopefully) make the job of overlap and deconfliction easier. Also, I for one favor using our intelligence apparatus to gather economic intelligence that U.S. businesses can use to stay ahead. America first.

16. If you had the chance to tell the warriors of the future one thing, what would it be?

BARENT: To trust your training and your instincts.

HARTOV: No matter the sophistication of the equipment, always remember that the human being is the key. Hone your personal skills, develop the seemingly redundant nuances, and you increase yours and your comrades' chances of victory and survival.

SCHNEIDER: Have a reason for being where you are.

STEWART: Mold a team with rigorous, realistic training and bring out individual strengths.

THOMPSON: Study your profession and don't let your desire to achieve a successful "career" interfere with the way you pursue your profession. Do what's right, not expedient, and do it well.

WALSH: We live in an age where technology is growing in leaps and bounds. The way we fight war is changing faster than doctrine can keep up with it. Despite these remarkable technological advances of today, we in the Special

Warfare business must still rely on our personal skill, intelligence, and courage to finish the job. Because when technology fails in the field (as it so often does), we, on the ground, operating isolated and alone, still won't have the option to quit. It will be the skill of each individual Special Warfare operator working in synch with the other team members to get there, to accomplish the mission, and to survive. We need to maintain our physical and mental standard and not give in to parity for the sake of economics or politics. As we are fond of saying in Naval Special Warfare, "The only easy day was yesterday."

Extra Credit

If there is a question you were hoping to answer that we didn't ask, state that question and answer it.

HARTOV: You asked a lot, and I've already said too much.

Editors' Epilogue

We add this commentary at the request of some of our contributors. That request stems from one of the attributes of this community that, to our knowledge, exists in no other similar group. Information circulates widely and fast among the cognoscenti; people feel it their duty to read, react, reason, and comment forthrightly; improvements are suggested without false humility and with arguments based on fact and principle.

This manuscript had been read by a number of highly qualified, extremely busy intellects among the Washington defense community before its editor of record in Connecticut called to say she had received our package. We had sent out only two manuscripts—one to a friend in D.C., and one to New York. The very day we learned that our package was safe in our editor's hands, our Washington friend called and asked for an appointment to see us—about the project.

He came to our office and stayed for an hour, discussing the reaction among his peers, and asking us to do this epilogue, which should, in the opinion of those responding through him, sum up what the text has shown us: argument, consensus, and summation. Also, our friend asserted, we should put a note in the text saying we valued the disparity in style, intellectual ability, and command of English virtually as voiced, as an additional feature of each commentary. Otherwise, said our friend, some readers might find it unnerving to read sequential pieces displaying such a range of intent, education, self-awareness, and articulation.

So herewith, the aforementioned note: we put it here, at the end, where we feel it will not prejudice the reader. We wanted to show the breadth of this community, for it is as diverse as America itself. We hoped for, and received, revealing commentary from every subcomponent of this hidden society that normally keeps only its own counsel. Our writers told us what they intended, and they told us much more.

They told us whom they respect, and it was seldom the same answer. They told us how they see themselves and their societies, and it was, more often than not, a story of worlds in collision. And yet they showed, one and all, an awareness of duty, a concern with the future, a broad grasp of international security issues, and a sense of elastic community that may not exist anywhere else in the United States.

These people have respect for one another, and for the institutions they serve, even when they are savagely critical of the failures of those institutions. They share, more than any other group we have ever encountered, a vision of America that resides in their hearts as well as in their heads. They understand democracy with a clarity seldom encountered among the civilian world—its demands can kill them, cripple them, keep them poor, dirty, hungry, and frustrated. They know from bitter experience that democracy, although it allows for excellence, inclines to mediocrity. And yet they are not bitter, on the whole.

As a group—or, let us once more say it, as a *class*—they are the keepers of the pragmatic hopes of our great experiment. Some wish that the Republic were not so democratic; some wish that excellence ruled among them, and, more fervently, among the greater country they serve. Some truly believe that excellence does still reside within our borders, that we are one nation, under God, indivisible—that God is still on our side. Freedom and justice are real to these people, who have given up so much freedom, and sometimes even their claim to justice, to keep alive the ideals that formed this country and informed the struggles of other countries toward those same ideals.

When we first came to Washington, we were fond of saying we were here to make the nation's capital safe for democracy. We don't say it much anymore—the struggle is endemic. Everyone here, consciously or unconsciously, is fighting the same fight.

We are reminded of that fight most clearly when any of us are abroad. When Romania freed itself from a tyrant in 1989, a group of U.S. experts went there on a fact-finding trip. One night in the house of a local resident many were brought to tears by the comment that Radio Free Europe, and then Voice of America radio programs, had been the greatest contributing factor to the revolution in that country.

At that same time in history, the people of Sophia would gather every night at ten P.M. in the town square—they were still afraid to gather in people's homes—and would sing an American song. That song was entitled, "Don't Worry, Be happy." Whether the people of Romania can find true freedom is up to them. Whether freedom will bring them happiness, only time will tell.

We have sent our message around the world, using space-based communications, radio waves, our national and natural resources, and the lives of our fighting men and women for generations. We have outspent and outmaneuvered the Soviet Union, and now find ourselves without a proper enemy in sight. Whether we can actually be what we were content becoming—the leader of the world—is up to us. Einstein said that the difference between Americans and Europeans was that Americans were concerned with becoming, Europeans with being. Must we now become something else, besides the beacon of democracy? Can we hold this mountaintop, or have we spent ourselves, like all great civilizations before us, attaining our heart's desire?

In the editors' secret hearts, we hoped that the answers to our questions, often formulated to be distressing, evocative, even taunting, would give us a clue to our national future. We think, looking back on this project and its results, that we have succeeded in large measure in what we set out to do.

Our reading of these documents tells us that, among those caretakers of our Constitutional heritage exists a group of people, embedded in and among those caretakers, who are comfortable being labeled "the warrior class." And that, around and among them, there are those who believe more fervently in the force of mind than in the force of body. Their contribution is one of moderation, and they are quick to refuse the stigma of "class" altogether, as they should when "social class" is what is meant. As we hope the United States can continue to do—A classless society is one of the ideals of our heritage.

We do not apologize for using the word *class* to stimulate debate, to lure some because of misunderstanding, some because of understanding, some because of identification, some because of revulsion, and some for the sheer intellectual joy of investigation. We have all kinds, in this volume. As does this nation.

This group is not homogeneous. Not in mind. Not in body. Not in deed or creed or motivation or reason. Except in one overriding way: in a society which has become overly concerned with material gain, with money as an end rather than a means, with personal profit and success above all, each of these people has elected a career that offers low pay, long hours, and few rewards in contemporary civilian terms. So for all the talk and argument in these pages, they are a class apart, a special group, a discrete subset.

If this book has been successful in revealing something about the American character, it is due to this sameness that guaranteed us an honesty and quality in response. Each agreed to contribute to this project for the pure satisfaction of a task well done, for the opportunity to contribute something, for the chance to voice their opinion, for the satisfaction of being part of a successful community endeavor. We don't believe that any other group of people within the United States could have been counted upon to respond to such a request. With gusto. With enthusiasm. With questions only about who else might be among their ranks. Without complaint about the limited recompense (one copy of the finished book given to each contributor).

So we are satisfied, by the fact that we have reached this point and compiled this volume, that we have proved our thesis. Call them what you will, this group is among us, and their values are different than the values of a group of lawyers, stockbrokers, entrepreneurs, or politicians. They have, at bottom, much more in common than in dispute. And the nature of their disputes will help create the future for us all.

The truth of each contributor's piece lies in great measure in the individuality of that person's voice, in the individual mode of expression, which tends to match, and even foretell, the scope of the concerns clearly shaping each contribution. Each writer has spoken from a vantage point, and those vantage points are so discrete, so compartmentalized, so much a product of the specialized training each has received, that we expect a certain amount of distress from opposite poles when the book is printed.

Some snake-eaters will grumble at the rigorously intellectual, ruthlessly reasoned pieces written by some senior analysts, and complain that those contributions are irrelevant to the real world and don't tell it like it is. Some intellectuals will be hard-put to credit the contributions of butt-in-the-mud soldiers as having any place in a volume with their deeply thought pieces, which would have been equally at home in scholarly journals. Some citizen-soldiers will be embarrassed by the machismo of the professional, even mercenary, fighters among our contributors. The techno-elite will take issue with the ground-pounder who believes that warriors are born, not made. The old-timers will worry about what the yuppies and the women are going to do to our fighting force. The generation who sees no difference between urban combat and guerilla warfare will confront the Special Forces people, who know that their lives hang on an understanding of that very crucial difference.

And there will be debate over whether any of all of the above can be tolerated by the others of strong opinion among their ranks—about whether so great a disparity of kind can be classed together. For that is the true meaning we ascribed to "class." For us, this exploration is one of sociology, of morphology, of trying to determine what comprises this set of persons grouped together by their actions—and not of a division or order of society.

We think that this exercise has proved that there is a warrior

class, self-chosen, set apart by its actions, by its ideals, by its sacrifices. We think that this classification overrides and overwhelms distinctions such as education, intellectual capability, and even societal differences. That is what we mean by "class." It is noteworthy that some understood this, and others did not, but ascribed the sinister connotations of "social class" to the title.

Perhaps, if we have done our jobs correctly in the compilation and introduction of these remarkable people, each of whom is as important to this contribution as is any other, the ensuing debates and phone calls and complaints and embarrassed laughter will give way in time to a deeper understanding that is as American as is our heritage and our values provided by the security of our Constitution.